Praise for
The True Source of Healing

"In a time when we have lost our collective and personal souls, Tenzin Wangyal offers us an unfailing compass to our original, unbroken self. Read this book, and find your way back to health and wholeness!"

— **Alberto Villoldo, Ph.D.**, author of
Shaman, Healer, Sage and *Mending the Past
and Healing the Future with Soul Retrieval*

"Tenzin Wangyal is a generous teacher, an insightful master, and a brilliant translator of timeless wisdom. In *The True Source of Healing*, he demystifies the ancient practice of soul retrieval in a profound, clear, and accessible way that gently leads us to the core of our very being. This journey with Tenzin is a joy, and the results are transformational."

— **davidji**, best-selling author of *Secrets of Meditation*

"Tenzin Rinpoche offers an ancient, lineage-based approach to the concept of soul retrieval, and in so doing brings brilliant Tibetan Bön wisdom to the heart of this practice."

— **Charlie Morley**, author of *Dreams of Awakening*

"What a treasure! Tenzin Wangyal Rinpoche skillfully guides us in ancient practices to retrieve our basic goodness and intelligence. These practices, which we can apply immediately to our fast-paced and stress-filled lives, will revitalize us at the deepest level of our being. *The True Source of Healing* invites us to stillness, silence, and spaciousness, and to joyfully allow the qualities of our basic nature— unbounded awareness and a warm heart— to emerge so that we may be healed."

— **Matteo Pistono**, author of *Fearless in Tibet* and
In the Shadow of the Buddha

the true
source of
healing

Also by Tenzin Wangyal Rinpoche

*Awakening the Luminous Mind**

*Awakening the Sacred Body**

Healing with Form, Energy, and Light

Tibetan Sound Healing

Tibetan Yogas of Body, Speech, and Mind

The Tibetan Yogas of Dream and Sleep

Unbounded Wholeness (with Anne Carolyn Klein)

Wonders of the Natural Mind

*Available from Hay House

PLEASE VISIT:

Hay House USA: www.hayhouse.com®
Hay House Australia: www.hayhouse.com.au
Hay House UK: www.hayhouse.co.uk
Hay House India: www.hayhouse.co.in

the true source of healing

How the Ancient Tibetan Practice
of Soul Retrieval Can Transform
and Enrich Your Life

TENZIN WANGYAL RINPOCHE

edited by Polly Turner

HAY HOUSE, INC.
Carlsbad, California • New York City
London • Sydney • New Delhi

Copyright © 2015 by Tenzin Wangyal

Published in the United States by: Hay House, Inc.: www.hayhouse.com® • **Published in Australia by:** Hay House Australia Pty. Ltd.: www.hayhouse.com.au • **Published in the United Kingdom by:** Hay House UK, Ltd.: www.hayhouse.co.uk • **Published in India by:** Hay House Publishers India: www.hayhouse.co.in

Cover design: Angela Moody | amoodycover.com
Cover illustration: Selver Serdar | freeimages.com
Interior design: Bryn Starr Best

Cataloging-in-Publication Data is on file at the Library of Congress

Tradepaper ISBN: 978-1-4019-4449-0

1st edition, July 2015

Printed in the United States of America

For my teacher,
Yongdzin Tenzin Namdak Rinpoche

Contents

Preface

I believe there is no better moment than now to introduce these practices of soul retrieval, which have so much power to help you connect with the natural environment, with others, and with your soul. Done daily, these practices have the potential to transform your life. They can help you come home to your inherent joy, reenergize your relationships, feel more connected and productive at work, and find healing for physical maladies, as well as bring happiness and well-being to others.

The wisdom in this book is very old. It has its source in Tibetan Bön Buddhism, the indigenous spiritual tradition of Tibet and one of the world's richest and most ancient unbroken spiritual traditions. The Bön soul-retrieval practices and rituals remain as alive and relevant today as they were well before Buddhism arrived in Tibet in the 7th century. However, since most Western students don't have time in their busy lives to learn complex rituals, in this book I am omitting explanations of the traditional ceremonies and rituals of soul retrieval and focusing instead on the most essential elements of the core teachings.[1]

While presenting the practices and their explanations in as simple and accessible a way as possible, I remain true to the ancient texts. My intention is to offer a clear path to solid experiences that can shift your energy and understanding toward healing and renewal, help you clear the negative thoughts and emotions that obstruct your happiness and well-being, and assist you in retrieving the enthusiasm and vitality you may have lost in life. Ultimately, the teachings presented here are about reconnecting deeply and completely with your soul, with your genuine nature, so that you can live a more authentic, balanced, and fulfilled life.

My own upbringing and training were very traditional. My father was a Buddhist lama and my mother a Bön practitioner. I was born in India soon after they escaped from Tibet during the Chinese Cultural Revolution. After my father passed away, my mother married a Bön lama. At age ten I entered Menri Monastery near Dolanji, India, now one of the two main Bön monasteries outside of Tibet. At the Dialectic School of Menri I spent 11 years as a monk engaged in a traditional, rigorous course of study toward a *geshe* degree. My studies included epistemology, cosmology, sutra, tantra, and dzogchen. I received my degree in 1986, and since then I have been living and teaching in the West. I currently live with my wife and son in Northern California.

From as early as I can remember, the drums, bells, and conch-shell horns of the traditional Bön rituals were part of my life, as familiar to me as video games are to children today. As a child, I was particularly impressed with the soul-retrieval ritual. In Tibet, soul-retrieval rituals are commonly recommended for patients who feel energetically drained but have been unable to obtain a clear diagnosis from a physician. My mother was seldom well, and after she had undergone many treatments, it was determined that her healing could be advanced only if elaborate ceremonies and soul-retrieval rituals were performed on her behalf. A traditional Tibetan view is that illness can be linked to soul loss and that one of the many causes of losing your soul is that the spirits are provoked because you have harmed their world. So the rituals for my mother involved creating harmony with the spirits, offering them what they needed to pacify them, and requesting that they stop damaging my mother's vitality and return what they had stolen from her. After one ceremony, my mother even changed her name as a way of releasing her identity as a sick person and taking on a new, healthier identity.

While this book contains none of the traditional Bön rituals, the guidance it offers is the heart essence of their healing powers. Tibetans typically refer to soul and life-force retrieval as *laguk tseguk,* with *la* meaning "soul," *guk* meaning "to retrieve" or "to call," and *tse* meaning "life force." The practices of soul retrieval not only provide healing for those who are sick or dying but also serve people who are physically healthy. They offer an excellent means of reinforcing your vitality on a daily basis. If you are feeling disconnected, these practices can help you find a sense of connection with yourself, with others, and with the world around you.

Like many other indigenous traditions, Bön emphasizes the need to heal the soul for the welfare of all human beings and the earth itself. This philosophy of healing oneself for others' welfare plays an important role in the Bön causal vehicles, the system of teachings that is the primary source of the soul-retrieval practices. Within Bön's vast system of knowledge, all of the principal teachings in its Southern Treasure tradition are categorized according to the Nine Ways of Bön, the first four of which are known as the causal vehicles. The causal vehicles focus on methods for working beneficially with the power and spirits of nature, as well as with astrology, divination, medicine, and cosmology. They provide a foundation for practicing Bön's higher vehicles of sutra, tantra, and dzogchen. Dzogchen is known as the vehicle of great perfection.

In my view, all of the Bön teachings are interconnected, and as reflected in the methods described in this book, all can play a role in healing the soul. Whether soul retrieval is done through communing with the elements of nature, through clearing negative emotions and cultivating positive qualities, or through connecting with subtle wisdom states in dzogchen practice, it points us toward the same experience: a deeper connection with the spacious awareness that is our authentic self, the source of all the positive qualities a human being needs to be joyful and fulfilled, and lead a life that benefits others.

ཀྱེ་ཡེ་ཡོན་ཏན་བསམ་ཡས་ཆེ། །

རྒྱལ་པོའི་གཏེར་ཁ་ཕྱེ་འདྲ་བས། །

ཀྱེ་དོན་གནས་ཡིན་གང་ཟག་དེ། །

འགུར་འབུ་ཆེ་འབྲས་གདོད་ནས་སྐྱེ། །

Its positive qualities are inconceivable,
Like the revelation of a king's treasure.
The one who rests within its true meaning
Enjoys the inexhaustible wealth of its fruition.

—from *The Seven Mirrors*
of Dzogchen, a Bön dzogchen text[1]

Introduction

I once did a television interview that began a bit awkwardly. When I arrived at the studio, the host was acting moody and distracted. He was shuffling papers and gulping his coffee, and it seemed like all he wanted was to be somewhere else. But as soon as he was cued that the show was about to go live, he sat up tall and with a big smile said brightly to the camera, "Good morning, everyone!" I was so surprised by his instant transformation that it took me a minute or two to relax into the interview.

We all know what a real smile looks like. It arises naturally from an open heart and comes with lightness, warmth, and spontaneous laughter. The eyes sparkle, the gaze connects. Few people who receive a genuine smile can help but smile back. But the smile of that TV host had nothing to do with authentic joy or liveliness. It was superficial and forced, and glossed over his bad mood. Clearly this man had learned how to switch on a big, bright smile, but not how to access genuine warmth as he did so.

How many of us dread going to work each morning? We may wear professional smiles all day and then carry our stress and unhappiness back home with us every evening. While we look like we have everything—a job, a home, a family—we may be feeling dark and depressed inside. We may be struggling to find happiness, never fully

7

satisfied with what we have. The sense of disconnectedness and dissatisfaction in today's society seems pervasive.
Many people lead active lives and accomplish a lot, and
yet it can be hard for any of us to recognize and reflect on
our pain and discontent, or understand what is causing it.

We are missing something essential that is actually
deep within us. Spontaneity, creativity, ease, and playfulness are qualities of our natural state of being, but we fail
to realize this. From the Tibetan Bön perspective, when we
lose the connection to our natural state, we lose our soul.
The good news is that we can fully retrieve what we have
lost. Recall a moment in your life when you felt complete,
satisfied, fully alive, at home in yourself. Imagine that it is
possible for you to feel that way not only now and then but
most of the time. This is what soul-retrieval practice offers.

What Is the Soul?

In the context of the Bön soul-retrieval practice, the
soul (la in Tibetan) is understood as the balance of the
subtle energies and related qualities of the five elements:
earth, water, fire, air, and space. The ancient Tibetan teachings tell us that everything in life—in fact, everything in
the universe and any experience we can have—is made up
of these five elements. Without the external elements of
soil, water, air, and the heat of the sun, we could not exist,
be sustained, or receive nourishment. Similarly, our soul
cannot remain nourished without the inner essences of
the five elements.

Our inner experience of these elemental qualities in-
cludes a sense of groundedness and connectedness (earth),
comfort and fluidity (water), joy and inspiration (fire), flexibility and movement (air), and openness and accommodation

(space). If one or more of these five natural elements is lacking or diminished in us, our soul will be damaged. When these qualities come into balance, it is said that our soul is healed. In the practice of soul retrieval, what we retrieve are these elemental qualities. It may be that you only need to retrieve a single quality in order to bring every other quality into balance.

Causes of Soul Loss

According to traditional Tibetan teachings, damage to your soul also diminishes your life force—your vitality. Soul loss can lead to physical weakness and illness. It can affect you emotionally, energetically, psychologically, and spiritually. In extreme cases, soul loss can lead to death. The imbalance of the elements related to soul loss is usually a result of the inevitable challenges we face in life. The challenges might be anything from an unhealed childhood trauma to a sudden shock, such as the unexpected death of a loved one. Soul loss can also happen gradually as a result of accumulated stress. Collectively, entire nations can suffer soul loss as a result of wars and natural disasters.

How do you know when your soul is injured or depleted? Often this is experienced as pervasive, chronic dissatisfaction. You might try to distract yourself by watching lots of television, surfing the Internet, mindlessly eating or drinking, or engaging in any number of other diversions, and yet the feeling of dissatisfaction is always in the background. While you cannot pinpoint the cause, you know that you are not happy.

A sense of exhaustion can be another sign of soul loss. Perhaps you are caring for an aging parent while juggling the demands of your own life. Your intention is to be compassionate and generous in all the right ways, but you feel stressed out and depleted. The problem is not the amount of time you are spending on helping another; it's that you are acting from a disconnected place. When we are connected to our natural state of being, giving to others involves no stress or mental exhaustion. Like a genuine smile, our actions are spontaneous, effortless, and joyful. They energize both the giver and the receiver.

But when we feel disconnected, there is a sense of lack, a sense of wanting or needing more for ourselves. Anything can seem wrong: where you are, what you are doing, whom you are with, how you feel in your body. You may feel a sense of loneliness or a lack of trust in yourself, in others, in your world. This chronic sense of needing more becomes your identity.

When soul loss is severe—for example, when it happens in connection with a major trauma—it can manifest as post-traumatic stress disorder (PTSD). People with PTSD may have recurring nightmares, flashbacks, or disabling anxiety, and have a hard time functioning in everyday life. Combat veterans and victims of violent crime are among those who may suffer from this severe loss of soul. It can also come from a traumatic event, like witnessing a terrible car accident, suddenly losing your job, or having a heart attack.[2]

A Path to Healing

No matter what has happened to you in life, or what type of pain you have, or how much or how little pain, the soul-retrieval practices in this book offer a direct way to address your suffering. Through these practices it is possible to clear the negative emotions and energies that are blocking your joyful nature and to retrieve and cultivate the elemental qualities that nourish you. The act of retrieving is essential for healing.

Chapter 1, Looking Closely at Your Life, helps you identify the element you need most at this time in order to heal your soul. Chapter 2, Retrieving from Nature, explains how to retrieve the element you need directly from the natural world. We retrieve it not only from the raw element, whether it is earth, water, fire, air, or space, but also from the subtler essence of that element. Water, for example, is not just the clear, life-giving liquid that flows through rivers and streams; water is also its qualities of fluidity, comfort, and ease. On an even deeper level, each element is associated with a different wisdom. Earth can be experienced as mirrorlike wisdom, or awareness that reflects all things in a nonjudgmental way. Through deep meditation practice you can connect with each element in its purest form, as a quality of light or luminous awareness.

Table 1. The five elements and their associated qualities, wisdoms, and pure lights

Element*	Basic qualities	Wisdom	Pure light
Earth	Groundedness, connectedness	Mirrorlike wisdom	Yellow
Water	Comfort, fluidity	All-accomplishing wisdom	Blue
Fire	Joy, inspiration	Discriminating wisdom	Red
Air	Flexibility, movement	The wisdom of equanimity	Green
Space	Openness, accommodation	The wisdom of emptiness	White

* To learn more about these elemental aspects, see Chapter 2, Retrieving from Nature.

Chapter 3, Retrieving by Taking Inner Refuge, points you to your inner refuge: the openness, awareness, and warmth of your authentic nature. This is the source of all the elemental essences. We refer to it as *refuge* because it is the only true source of comfort, relief, and support. Normally, when facing difficulties in life, we seek refuge in people, places, and things outside of us—for example, we depend on a friend's advice or on finding a different job or place to live to resolve our problems or make us feel better. But any external source of support is impermanent by nature and is sure to be lost to us one day. The inner refuge is also the source of loving-kindness, compassion, joy, and equanimity—known as the four immeasurables—as well as all other virtuous qualities. The meditation practice described in Chapter 3 helps you enter this refuge through the three doors of body, speech, and mind.

Chapter 4, Retrieving from Relationships, explains how, through the practice of inner refuge, you can retrieve the elements lost in your interactions with loved ones and in other significant relationships. Chapter 5, Overcoming Loneliness, highlights loneliness as a pervasive human suffering that is yet another aspect of soul loss, and discusses how you can heal it by reconnecting to the source within.

Chapter 6, Nourishing Your Inner Being, and Chapter 7, Nourishing Your Physical Body, go to the heart of soul retrieval, emphasizing the importance of routinely nourishing yourself at all levels. You can look at nourishing as keeping your internal battery charged. In today's fast-paced, industrialized, technological lifestyle, many of us are losing pieces of our soul every day. We can be drained by the challenges of a daily commute, juggling family and work obligations, even noise pollution. When we recognize how frequently we are drained, we can find opportunities to reconnect to the inner refuge and recharge every day. Chapter 6 offers guidance for nourishing your inner being. Chapter 7 explains how to use certain practices to ease physical pain and even prevent or heal disease.

Each chapter closes with a series of actions you can take. Included are instructions for formal practice (the time you set aside each day to sit undisturbed in meditation) and informal practice (bringing what you learn from your formal meditation into your daily life).

For additional support in your practice, I have recorded a guided meditation focused on the practice of Retrieving by Taking Inner Refuge. To access this recording, visit www.hayhouse.com/download and enter the Product ID 2190 and download code ebook. If you have any trouble accessing the meditation audio, please contact Hay House Customer Care by phone—US (800) 654-5126 or INTL CC+(760) 431-7695—or visit www.hayhouse.com/contact.

The Best Remedy

Soul retrieval involves inner work. A common response to troubling thoughts and feelings is to either push them away or distract yourself. But when you try to deaden your thoughts and feelings, they just become more insistent. There's much to be gained from noticing difficult feelings, listening to them, and in certain instances, expressing them.

However, if you dwell on your thoughts and feelings, one thought almost always leads to another, which inevitably reinforces the pain. The mind that is in pain cannot think its way out of its pain. As a traditional Tibetan saying goes, you cannot remove blood from your hands by washing them with more blood. I call the mind that tries to think its way out of pain the "smart ego." It is often difficult to recognize the smart ego for what it is, because we are continually giving ourselves advice that seems positive, attractive, and solution oriented. The smart ego can be a frequent guest at our meditation sessions, mixing itself into our moments of insight and proclaiming itself as wisdom. But this so-called wisdom is not the result of true self-reflection. It is an obstacle to true wisdom, to recognizing the nature of mind.

Another way we try to overcome our problems is by expressing them in a journal or to a friend, counselor, or therapist. This can put us more in touch with difficult emotions so they can be worked through and released. There is clearly a place for psychotherapy in healing, but I wonder if people are talking about their problems from the right space. Many spend years in therapy or support groups talking about the same issues over and over, unable to transform their suffering because they lack higher awareness.

How can we access higher awareness? By taking what I call the three precious pills—stillness, silence, and spaciousness—which connect us to the inner refuge. From this unbounded sacred space, if we recall our negative emotions or other painful experiences and host them without judging, criticizing, rejecting, or grasping them, we engage the process of healing. By hosting, I mean allowing the pain to freely arise, abide, and dissolve. This experience is like being a gracious host who allows guests to come as they are, stay as long as they wish, leave when they're ready, and even return. Hosting pain in this way allows it to fully dissolve into the sacred space of the inner refuge, which gives rise to awareness that is fresh and creative.

What truly sets these practices of soul retrieval apart from most forms of therapy is that the primary work begins once the pain subsides. It is common for people who succeed in overcoming pain and conflict to think *Okay, now I'm clear of this problem. Good riddance!* and then look for the next problem to solve. They clear a space for the next problem to arise, and so it does! But when we move from one problem to the next, we do not cultivate familiarity with the presence of awareness of the space that is free of pain. This space is the source of the qualities that are natural antidotes to the pain. When, through awareness, we connect to this space, we receive nourishment.

Sometimes it's better not to think and talk so much. For it is only when we can be with our pain fully and host it from the space of the stillness of the body, silence of speech, and spaciousness of mind that we can connect with infinite awareness and warmth, from which healing qualities naturally arise. It is only from the space of openness that the disturbing emotions can be fully acknowledged and released, and the soul retrieved. When the soul is restored, there is greater continuity to our happiness.

Therapeutic Meditation

I have long been curious about the relationship between psychotherapy and meditation practice. Perhaps people engage in years of psychological work without considering it a part of their spiritual development—they see it only as handling the problems in their lives. While they may be getting closer to an authentic sense of who they are, if their goal is primarily to resolve their problems, they miss a higher opportunity. In many religious groups, there are devoted practitioners who engage deeply in prayer and ritual without necessarily touching their personal issues. They may practice beautifully, sitting in meditation for hours with the highest of aspirations, wishing the best for humankind and all beings, but their practice bypasses their poor self-image or the disappointment they feel in their relationships.

For me, practicing meditation and resolving personal problems go hand in hand. Real meditation practice should be therapeutic practice. It should touch on and address your immediate personal issues. The one who is seeking happiness, freedom, a sense of connection, and even enlightenment is the one affected by those personal issues.

In the ancient dzogchen tradition of Tibet, the highest form of meditation is to abide in the nature of mind. When you do the simple core practice of inner refuge as described in Chapter 3 and rest in your mind's true nature, you have the opportunity not only to clear emotions and overcome personal challenges, but also to connect with the elemental essences that can heal your soul and support you in realizing the nature of mind. It is not necessary to engage in many different rituals, prayers, and visualizations to retrieve your soul. Experiencing and becoming familiar with the nature of mind during a single meditation session illuminates the path to realization.

ཀུ་ག་ཤུ་ན་རྩ་ག་ག་ཁ་ལ་ཞེ་ལ་རྗེ། །

རེ་ཡ་ཁྱུ་ལ་ཟ་ཚག་ག་ཉེ་ཁྲེན། །

སྲི་ཞེ་ཞེ། །ག་ལ་རྗེ་ཁྲེ་ན་ཀྱུ་ས། །

ཚ་རྗེ་ཁྲེ་སྲེ་ག་ལ་རྗེ་ཁྲུ་ག་ཡ་ཟ་ར་ཀ །

The treasure of the sky, the perfect source-of-all,

Becomes obscured through the
successive layering of stains.

If there is no portal, it will not be seen.

Opening the door to the treasure reveals
the source of the treasure.

—from *The Twenty-One Nails,*
a Bön dzogchen text[1]

CHAPTER 1

Looking Closely at Your Life

Last year, soon after my family and I moved to Northern California, I went for a walk to the Berkeley Marina along the San Francisco Bay. Enjoying the fresh air and sparkling light, I gazed up at the sky. All of a sudden I felt a strong experience of openness, a feeling of being closely in touch with my inner sacred space. Spontaneous tears arose. I felt that nature was helping me recognize the inner treasure of my being, my true self. Through the doors of my senses, the natural environment supported me in making that connection.

Since that day, I've been going regularly for walks and bike rides in that area. As I do, I observe the walkers, joggers, and cyclists coming toward me. Some of these people seem to be having experiences similar to mine. From the joy radiating from their smiles, I sense that there is no other place they would rather be. But there are so many others who look like they don't want to be there. I can see in their faces that they are not fully present. Maybe their doctors told them to exercise, or they feel some other need or duty to do so. They seem distracted and unhappy, in the wrong place and the wrong space.

I wonder how the same environment can be so nourishing to some and have no impact on others. Furthermore, why do so many of us look for happiness, joy, peace, and comfort in all the wrong places? We seek refuge in bad relationships or toxic work environments, or in acquiring more stuff. In reality, we can find happiness, joy, peace, and comfort in connecting with the elements of nature. What nature gives is absolutely free of charge. But sadly, some of us lack the presence of heart and mind to receive the healing gifts that nature offers.

What happens when you spend an hour with someone who is complaining continually about their life? Their negativity creeps into your consciousness. You close down. What happens when you sit for an hour gazing at the clear, open sky? If you look at the sky only from a conventional perspective, you are likely to feel tired or spacey. But if you use this time to cultivate a sacred relationship with the space element, gazing at the sky can open and free you.

In the Bön tradition, there are yogis who spend hours at a time gazing at the sky in meditation. Their aim is to access the deep wisdom of an open heart and ultimately to embody that openness. Gazing at the sky can introduce you to your inner wisdom, the boundless and unchanging space of being, and this can transform your life.

Time for Self-Reflection

Some people miss the opportunity to connect with that sense of openness, but having a deeper connection with the space element can be quite fulfilling. Others may be missing the inspiration of fire in their work life, or the ease of water in their family life. What is missing for you? Where in your life do you feel something is missing? I encourage you to reflect upon this. Look closely at your life and identify what you most need.

You can begin by looking at four areas: personal alone time, family life, work life, and your connection to nature. In any of these areas, are you lacking a sense of stability, comfort, inspiration, flexibility, or openness? Notice any feelings of discomfort, sadness, exhaustion, or disconnection. I highly recommend doing the self-assessments in this chapter before trying any of the practices in the book, so that you can focus on the issue that's most important to you in ways that will bring real results.

Look at Your Personal Life

Do you feel at home within yourself? One way to reflect on this is to notice how often you need to be distracted. Do you fill your free time by going online, texting, watching television, or napping? Can you go for a walk, lie on the beach, or take a drive without listening to music or talking on your cell phone?

Reflect on the last time you were with a stranger. At the time, perhaps you noticed a slight sense of restlessness, tightness, or discomfort in your body or your breathing. If you feel that same lack of ease when you're alone, perhaps it's because you don't truly know yourself, and are therefore uncomfortable being by yourself.

I know a woman who is always doing chores and caring for her young son but never takes time for herself. Even when her child has a playdate and she is free to do anything she wants, she feels she has to catch up on housework. Home could be a source of nourishment and healing for her, but like many people, she finds it hard to be still even in her own home. It's as if our dishes are saying, "Clean me!" And so we move this cup from here to there, and that plate from there to here. Ask yourself: How do you feel when you are by yourself? Do you feel comfortable, connected, and renewed in the stillness, silence, and spaciousness? Or do you feel restless or listless? Maybe you have a negative self-image and seldom find a nourishing space within yourself. Recognizing your discomfort with yourself is the first step in the healing process.

Look at Your Family Life

Our family can provide a sense of belonging, a foundation that supports and nourishes our life. Some people are fortunate to have a stable, loving family. But this is not true for many of us. The pressures of divorce, alcoholism, financial difficulties, health issues, or a child's chronic behavior problems can pose serious challenges to the well-being of families. And when there is any change in the family dynamic, whether through marriage, birth, adoption, or death, every family member is affected.

Imagine a man whose mother is chronically depressed, and no matter how much he tries to help her, she pushes him away every time. He can't stop thinking about her unhappiness, and at the same time he can't process it, digest it, or deal with it. Thinking about it drains him. His whole life seems affected by it. It depletes his soul.

A woman moves in with a man who at first seems trusting, loving, and giving. Then he grows jealous, angry, and possessive, and starts to physically abuse her. Before this relationship, she experienced a lot of warmth when she was with people, and she was very much in touch with her creativity. Since entering into that relationship, she is no longer open and spontaneous, and has lost her trust in others and even herself.

The death of a loved one can be devastating. During a soul-retrieval workshop, a student told me that she finally understood the impact of losing her grandfather. Her grandfather had been more important to her than her parents, she explained. He had been like a father, mother, friend—everything. When she lost him, she lost her grounding quality, both in herself and in her relationships with men.

Sometimes collective family pain comes down through the generations. But when one person has the strength, confidence, and knowledge to recognize and be open to this collective family pain, it is possible to cultivate love and harmony, and break the cycle. The soul-retrieval practices offer such an opportunity.

While our stories may be different, their effect on us may be similar. Like many people, you may feel as if your family relationships deplete you instead of nourish you. Recognizing depletion is the first step in soul retrieval—you need to know what is missing before you can retrieve it. In this case, it's recognizing how your family lives in you.

Look at Your Work Life

Some people are passionate about their work; others are at least satisfied with their jobs. But many others don't like going to work each day. A recent Gallup poll found that more than half of all employees in the United States are not truly engaged at work: basically, they show up but aren't inspired by what they're doing. One in five workers is unhappy enough with their jobs to share their discontent with others.[2] Doing something you dislike 40 hours a week is likely to affect you deeply.

On any given Monday morning, you can sense the collective pain of your fellow commuters. You can see it in their facial expressions or hear it in their tone of voice. When a customs official asks an international traveler, "Are you traveling for work or pleasure?" the question itself assumes that work is not pleasurable.

Imagine a health aide who spends the day dealing with patients who are suffering mentally or physically, and instead of being energized by the services he performs, feels exhausted and stressed. Every moment of his day is draining. He carries this burden home each night, and the pain spills over into other areas of his life.

Ask yourself: Do you look forward to working each day? Do you feel energized and enlivened by your work? Do you feel bored, or stuck in a dead-end job? Once again, recognition is the first step in soul retrieval. Reflect on how your job lives in you.

Look at Your Relationship with Nature

If you are fortunate, you have an intimate knowledge of the sacred and restorative power of nature. This connection may stem from a childhood spent playing in woods and streams, backpacking in the mountains, or vacationing by the ocean. But for many of us, our world revolves around technology and social interplay. We feel most alive amid the hum of modern life, and when not engaged or busy, we feel numb or disoriented. The inner space that resonates vividly with the natural world is unfamiliar to many of us, especially city dwellers.

When was the last time you experienced the unbounded spaciousness of a clear, starry night sky, the clarity of sunlight reflecting on water, the immensity of a mountain, the ease and flow of a meandering river, the warmth of a campfire, or the playfulness of a spring breeze? You may enjoy spending time in a café watching people come and go, feeling warmth and liveliness supported by the pleasant aroma of coffee, but when was the last time you experienced the liveliness and power of the wilderness? Connection to the peaceful, joyful experience of who you are is directly accessible through the sights, sounds, smells, and textures of nature.

Once again, recognizing the presence or absence of this source of nourishment is the first essential step in healing soul loss. Ask yourself: How do you relate to the natural elements? Do you regularly take time to replenish yourself in nature? Is the natural world as lively for you as a coffee shop? Or is nature divorced from your inner world? If so, when did you lose your sacred connection to the natural world? Can you remember a time before you lost that connection? How did that feel?

The Five Elements

As you look at these four areas of your life—personal, family, work, and relationship with nature—you may notice that similar issues affect not just one but several facets of your life. For example, a lack of flow or creativity at work may show up in your family or personal life as well. Notice this. Bring to mind specific times and places where you felt something positive was lacking. How long have you been living with the feeling that something is missing? Once you become more intimate with that feeling, you can start to identify more precisely the quality that is lacking and discern what the antidote would be.

Usually we get caught up in stories we tell ourselves about people we're in conflict with or situations we dislike, but perhaps you could look at your problems in a whole new way. The work of soul retrieval is not so much about changing your external world, such as switching to a better job or trying to convince your partner to stop leaving dishes in the sink. It is about changing yourself. Soul retrieval has everything to do with discovering the space within, and then retrieving one or more of the five elemental essences that you lack and nourishing yourself from this source.

Which of the five elemental essences do you most need to nourish your soul? Having reflected upon the different areas of your life—personal, family, work, and nature—now explore which of the elements is most unbalanced in you.

Your Relationship with Earth

Intuitively, we are all familiar with what the earth element feels like. The quality of earth is a sense of groundedness, a feeling of being connected and centered. Earth supports the ability to connect with our thoughts, feelings, and emotions; with the people we care about; and with the work we do.

Maybe you know someone who always seems to be confident, stable, and grounded: this is a person with a healthy balance of the earth element. On the other hand, people with too little earth might seem flighty, spacey, agitated, without anchor. They may find themselves searching for something or someone to help them feel more stable and secure. People with too little of the earth element may have trouble completing what they begin.

At a subtler level, the earth element is associated with a feeling of being grounded in each moment just as we are. Imagine how the earth feels beneath your feet when you walk in the sand or stand on a rocky promontory. Can you imagine sinking roots into the earth like a tree? Take a moment to feel the support of the earth.

How secure do you feel in yourself? How often do you feel centered, with a real sense of connection to your work, friends, family, and the natural world? Do you regularly experience insecurity or agitation? If you have been feeling disconnected or ungrounded, where in your life do you most notice these feelings manifesting? Are feelings of disconnection a longstanding pattern in your life? What seems to trigger them?

Your Relationship with Water

Water offers a sense of comfort. When the water element is balanced in you, you are comfortable in your body and in your environment, comfortable at work and with your family. You are fluid, able to respond with ease to changing circumstances. Put simply, you enjoy life. In its higher dimension, a healthy connection with the water element brings an innate joy of being—a joy that is not dependent on whom you are with, what job you have, how much money you make, or other external circumstances.

When the water element is not balanced, you may feel ill at ease. Something seems off or not quite right. You can't get comfortable with yourself, your relationships, your job, your connection to nature. You lack a feeling of well-being.

Imagine hearing a gentle rain or feeling the flow of warm water over your body as you shower. Take a moment to experience the comfort and ease of water.

Do you tend to feel at peace, content, and comfortable in yourself and your world? Or are those feelings missing from your life? If they're missing, in what circumstances do you experience the lack? Is this a fundamental discomfort you feel even when alone? How long have you experienced this discomfort in your life—is it a longstanding pattern?

Your Relationship with Fire

While the water element is related to contentment, the fire element brings an enthusiastic joy that is mentally wakeful and physically blissful. When the fire element is balanced in you, not only are you full of creative ideas but you can initiate projects and bring them to fruition. You feel inspired in your work. Whether alone or with others, you are engaged with life.

When the fire element is blocked, you experience a lack of energy, inspiration, and vitality. Your life can seem like a plodding routine. Even if you have a good idea, your projects don't get off the ground.

Imagine enjoying the dance of a lively bonfire. Do you feel a spark of that kind of liveliness when you engage with life? If not, your everyday life might be causing you to lose the qualities of fire. Where do you feel this loss? In your family? At work? In your relationship with yourself? How long have you experienced a lack of enthusiasm in your life?

Your Relationship with Air

Imagine standing in an open field or a park, feeling the fresh wind play around you. There is a sense of freedom and flexibility in connecting with the air element. The air element is all-pervasive. As air moves, it disperses the clouds to reveal the open sky. In its subtler state, air clears away our discursive thoughts, revealing the cloudless inner sky of the mind.

When the air element within you is well balanced, you can readily transform negative mind states into positive ones—hate into love, pessimism into optimism, gloom into joy. You easily resolve worries and concerns. There is a playfulness about you. Even while you're going through a difficult time, you can still savor a good meal or a beautiful sunset. You are able to see things from varying perspectives and think in new ways. Air has to do with curiosity and discovery. Obstacles become opportunities for learning.

When air is not balanced, you feel stuck. Your career seems to be going nowhere, your relationships are not deepening, your meditation practice is not progressing, and you are not growing personally. There is no movement in your life.

Reflect on where you most sense a lack of freedom and flexibility. Do you feel constrained by the conditions of your life? Are you weighed down by family issues or ongoing conflict with your boss, or a weak or negative sense of self? How long has this lack of movement been present in your life?

Your Relationship with Space

The space element is the openness of the clear, cloudless sky. If the space element is balanced in you, whatever arises in your life can be accommodated. Even if you are working full time and juggling family responsibilities, there is room enough for it all. With your vast and accommodating perspective, you never seem to be overwhelmed by your experiences or tempted to sidestep your responsibilities.

Every pleasant experience reflects the presence of openness. Why are you enjoying a nice conversation with someone? Because you are open to that person. Why do you fall in love? Because you are open to a relationship. Why are you able to close an important deal at work, have fun with your children, or forgive someone who hurt you? Because you are open to the possibility. Even the deepest wounds can be healed when you open to the healing process. Ultimately, openness is the greatest support. Full integration with the space element results in the highest spiritual attainment: recognition of your true nature.

Conversely, the discomforts we experience often come from a lack of connection to the space element. With too little space, every challenge seems solid and impenetrable. When you lose something, like a job or a significant relationship or a home you love, you are bereft and can focus only on what is missing from your life.

The space element supports us in seeing possibilities, in expanding our horizons. Imagine the presence of a clear, cloudless sky. Take a moment to enjoy the spaciousness and reflect on these questions: Are you able to accommodate what is happening in your life, to make decisions and take action with confidence? Or, when difficulties arise, do you find yourself reacting impulsively and emotionally? Is work overwhelming? Are your children too much to handle? Do you seem not to have enough personal time? How long have you felt the lack of space in your life?

Table 2. Which element do you need?

Element	When the element is balanced, you	When you have too little, you	When you have too much, you	Possible cause of overabundance
Earth	Feel grounded, stable, connected, able to focus, strong, steady; have joy of being	Feel ungrounded, unstable, dissatisfied, disconnected, spacey, agitated, ever-searching, restless	Feel dull, lazy, unable to move, insensitive, stubborn, depressed, withdrawn, fixed; you tend to oversleep	Too little fire or air
Water	Feel comfortable, fluid, clear, peaceful, gentle, at ease, caring, loving, compassionate, calm, flowing, cleansed	Lack well-being, feel out of tune with yourself, feel as if something is "off"	Feel lost in comfort, unproductive, content with unfavorable situations, unaware of your emotions	Too little fire or air
Fire	Feel joyful, inspired, creative, enthusiastic, good-humored, strong-willed, powerful, quick, energetic, warm, blissful, orgasmic; you have experiences of ripening	Lack energy, vitality, enjoyment, or enthusiasm; you feel uninspired; you have, difficulty initiating or completing things	Feel agitated, restless, intolerant, quickly irritated, unstable; you have difficulty sleeping, being in silence, controlling thoughts	Too little water or earth

| Air | Feel flexible, free-moving, healing, lively, light, fresh, penetrating, magical, transformative, communicative | Feel stuck, feel a lack of flow, feel that you are not progressing or expanding, feel that your relationships are not deepening | Have trouble sticking to things; feel a lack of comfort and satisfaction in where you are, what you have, or what is; you are readily tossed about by external influences | Too little water or earth |
| Space | Feel open, accommodating, spacious, expansive, vast, pervasive, flexible, joyful | Feel blocked, lost, lacking openness; challenges seem solid and impenetrable | Feel disoriented, lost, disjointed, disconnected, out of touch, ungrounded, unable to prioritize | Too little earth |

Reflecting on What You Have Too Much Of

From the lists of qualities in and out of balance in Table 2, it may be immediately obvious which element you most need to retrieve. If not, you may be able to determine which element you lack by considering which one you have too much of. The elements exist in a dynamic relationship, so when one element becomes deficient, another becomes dominant.

Too much earth may indicate a deficiency of fire or air. When you have too much earth, instead of feeling grounded, connected, and confident, you may feel dull and lazy, unable to move. You may be surrounded by clutter. Problems seem solid, leaving you feeling stuck or resigned. You may feel insensitive, uninspired, or depressed. You may want to sleep a lot, and you may drift off while meditating.

Yet another sign of too much earth is not being fully engaged with life. The negative aspect of earth, according to the ancient texts, is ignorance of our true nature, one of the destructive emotions at the root of our suffering.

Too much water may indicate too little fire or air. When water is dominant, you may go out of your way to avoid discomfort. You may avoid responsibilities, even if it means giving up something you value. You may feel content or be overly accommodating in situations that call for action. With too much water, you easily become lost in your emotions. In meditation practice, an overabundance of water leads to a loss of clarity.

Too much fire is often a sign of too little water or earth. When fire dominates, you may be quickly irritated, agitated, or annoyed—you lack the comfort of water. You may react impulsively and be intolerant of other people's ways of acting, thinking, and being. Too much fire without the stability of earth can make you feel ungrounded, unstable, and restless. You may have difficulty sleeping, sitting still, or being in silence. You may speak rapidly and talk a lot, generating one idea after another without being able to fully articulate any of them. In meditation practice, too much fire can manifest as restlessness or agitation, and an abundance of intrusive thoughts.

Too much air may indicate too little earth or water. You may have trouble sticking with anything or accepting things as they are. If you have an abundance of air, no matter what situation you're in, something else looks better. You lack satisfaction with whatever or whoever is in your life. Ungrounded, lacking earth, you are easily thrown off balance by external influences.

Too much space may indicate too little earth. You become spacey, disjointed, and out of touch with what's going on around you. Because your experience of space lacks awareness, you lose connection with your true nature and therefore with all other elements.

Too much of any given element may also indicate a need to retrieve the space element. Without enough space, it is likely that another element will exert too much influence on how you react. When you are open and spacious, you come into balance more easily. Your mind is clearer, you feel less tension, and you respond rather than react to life circumstances—you make considered choices rather than acting without thinking.

Upon reflection, you may discover that you lack the qualities of more than one element. However, I recommend that you focus on retrieving just one element, because retrieving that element may be enough to bring you into balance. For example, if the sudden death of a loved one has disconnected you from the enthusiasm of fire, this may also result in disconnection from the comfort of water or the openness of space. However, retrieving the fire element may be all you need to heal the imbalance.

The Next Step: Committing to Change

You begin the process of soul retrieval by acknowledging that something is missing in your life, becoming familiar with the elements and their interactions, and then using that knowledge to pinpoint which element you need most.

Do you recognize a lack of vitality or well-being in your life? The second step in soul retrieval is to be aware of that lack, to know that lack is not your natural condition, and to make a commitment to change your experience of yourself and your life.

Which element is deficient in your life and most needed? Reflect deeply on this lack. Can you feel it in your body, in the rhythm of your breath, in your mind and heart? Without getting caught up in the stories surrounding this lack, become more familiar with the associated feelings, hosting them without judging or criticizing yourself or your experience. Remember that how you feel now may change as you engage the positive elemental quality you are missing.

The process of soul retrieval will reconnect you with the inner source of light and well-being that is your true nature. In making a clear commitment to connect with this inner source, find the voice that is true for you. Perhaps the words will be something like:

I recognize that I am suffering from a lack of [NAME OF ELEMENT] in my life. I commit to connecting more deeply with the source within and engaging with it to retrieve that element.

As you work with the practices in this book, focus on the element that you have identified as lacking. Give yourself enough time to experience success in the practice. Signs of success might be discovering that you feel more connected at work, that a relationship has transformed, that you have a more positive self-image, or that you have reconnected with nature. You may discover that the success you achieve extends beyond the specific area you have been focusing on. Feeling more connected at work, for example, might also help you feel more connected with your family.

The next three chapters offer practices for taking in nourishment from various sources: nature, the inner refuge, and relationships. You may find that one practice works better for you than the others, but I recommend that you try them all. You will come to know which practice you need at a particular time.

There is wisdom within you that is so much more resourceful and kind than the smart ego, which has been trying to solve your problems all by itself. Doing the practices in this book can help you open to this higher wisdom. As you develop a sense of openness, trust, and connection to something wiser than your ego, your respect for—even devotion to—the source within will further support success on your path.

ཀྱེ་ནི་པ་གདེ་ལ་ཤ་པ་འདི་ག་པ་ལ་ཡེ་ག་ཀྲ་ག་ལེ་བ། །

།ཤེ་ག་ལ་ར་ཕ་པ་གདེ་དེ་ཤ་ག་ལེ་ག་ལ་ཨ། །

ཀུ་ག་གཱི་ཀྱི་པ་བ་ཟུ་དེ་ག་ཡ་ཡ་ར་ཚ་ག་འདཿ། །

A person profoundly fearing birth and death,

In a delightful solitary retreat hermitage,

Should recognize the base-of-all and gain

deep certainty in innate self-awareness.

—from *The Twenty-One Nails,*
a Bön dzogchen text

CHAPTER 2

Retrieving from Nature

Experiencing the natural world as sacred is a source of nourishment for the soul. Connecting with the elements and retrieving one's soul in this way is an honored approach in Bön. When the sacred relationship with nature is cultivated, true healing is supported.

What is a sacred relationship with nature? I define as sacred anything that brings you closer to yourself, to recognizing the truth of who you are. Imagine two people who visit the mountains for very different reasons. One is a shaman, the other a mountain climber. The shaman approaches the mountain to consciously weaken his ego and strengthen his connection with his inner wisdom. The athlete approaches the mountain as a challenge to conquer. While the mountaineer may be immersed in nature and feel excited and stimulated as he climbs, in relishing achievement he unconsciously feeds his ego. By experiencing his worth as something that can be measured and attained, he is disconnecting from himself. His relationship with nature is not a sacred one.

You can experience nature as a teacher constantly transmitting knowledge and wisdom to you, or simply as a place to engage your ego. When you enter into a sacred relationship with nature, qualities of the elements awaken within you, and you discover and connect with your genuine self.

Tibetan Roots

Traditionally, the ancient practice of soul retrieval involves cultivating a sacred relationship with the spirits of nature. The idea of nature spirits may not fully resonate with you, but knowledge of this perspective can help to increase your understanding and motivation for change, because it enters you into a relationship with the natural world that is dynamic and alive.

Like many indigenous cultures, the Tibetans consider the forces of nature to be alive with unseen beings.[1] To Tibetans, cultivating a relationship with the spirit of a tree or rock or stream is no less important than honoring human relationships. When you connect with the liveliness in nature, you are not lonely. Relaxing in front of a fire and feeling its warmth, you become aware of the spirit of the fire. Sitting by a river, you can form a relationship with the water spirits. Developing a deeper level of closeness, communication, and respect for an element and its spirit helps you awaken the essence of that element within you.

Making a Date with the Elements

A friend of mine, feeling old and sick, made a point upon arising each morning to sit on her porch and look at the sky and listen to the birds. This simple addition to her morning routine made the rest of her day go more smoothly. It left her feeling more open. On the mornings she didn't do it, she could feel the difference. Being with the sky didn't involve any complicated meditation postures, visualizations, or mantras, yet it awakened the healing qualities of her inner spaciousness. In a direct way, this illustrates the way nature can nourish us.

Making a special date with the elements is something anyone can do, yet few people think of doing it. It is a matter of finding the time and place to be with the elements and feel their liveliness.

When making a date with nature, you can be assured that, unlike some of your friends and relatives, nature will not judge you, try to convince you of anything, or expect anything of you. To make the connection, all that is required of you is to be still within yourself, silence your internal chatter, and open your heart. If you can rest in stillness, silence, and spaciousness, you will be open to receiving what nature has to offer.

If you have been feeling that your problems are solid and overwhelming, go to a place where the space element is evident. This might be a mountain overlook, a broad field, or a tall building with a window view. Choose a day when the sky is clear and a time when the sun is not directly in your eyes.

When you can connect long enough, gazing at a clear sky can open your heart and mind, and awaken an experience of inner spaciousness. It can bring you home to who you are, to the true nature of your mind. By the end of your session with the space element, all the challenges that have been weighing on you may seem lighter. You may feel better able to accommodate whatever arises in your life.

So, just as my friend did, consider spending quality time with the space element in a place where the sky is open and clear. Whether you travel to an open area or simply look out your window, use the time to connect with and nurture a feeling of openness.

If you have been feeling stuck and are in need of the air element, you can seek out a windy location. Go to a spot where people fly kites. Consider a high point, such as a hilltop or mountain pass, or visit the beach. In our daily lives there are many opportunities to experience the air element. You can connect with it anywhere the wind blows free—even on a city street. The skyscrapers in a city like New York create a wind-tunnel effect. As the wind blows around you, become aware of your inner playfulness and flexibility.

It's a Tibetan tradition to toss thin papers containing prayers into the breeze, imagining that the air disperses the prayers throughout the universe. The purpose of this ritual is to raise your *windhorse,* your life force. A mythical Tibetan creature, the windhorse symbolizes the space element, the subtle energy of inner air. It brings good fortune, ensuring that every circumstance you meet will lead to your success and well-being. As the wind lifts your prayers into the sky, your inner wind raises your energy. You can explore this connection between the outer and inner winds in your practice. The more you connect with the wind element and merge with its qualities, the more flexible and resilient you will be. You will feel yourself opening to new perspectives and will sense your potential for expansion and growth.

If you have been lacking energy, vitality, or inspiration and are in need of the fire element, find a place where fire is active. Sit by a campfire or a fireplace, enter a sweat lodge, or simply light candles. A good way to connect with fire is to sit in the sun and feel your skin absorbing its warmth. In Northern Europe, after the long, dark winter, people congregate outdoors to celebrate the return of the sun's rays. There is even more power in remaining aware as you actively engage with the fire element.

The point is not to become so absorbed in the fire that you lose yourself but rather, through connecting with fire's energetic warmth, to find yourself. As you become more receptive to and engaged with the qualities of fire, feelings of joy are likely to replace sadness and depression. In your innermost being, you *are* joy. Fire awakens this in you. Even when the flames subside or the sun disappears behind a cloud, the warmth and joy remain.

Make an appointment with the fire element. Whether you sit by a campfire or in a sunny spot by a window, feel fire's blissful vitality arising within you.

If you have been experiencing a lack of ease and you need the water element, look for a place where water is active. Spend time by a lake or waterfall, canoe or tube on a river, swim or float in a pond or pool, ride on a ferry, or walk in the rain. Wherever water is, go there and be with it, engage with it. Can you feel the water energy flowing throughout your body, cleansing and healing it? Can you feel the stiffness of your planning mind relax? As you soften your body and breathe, can you feel that you *are* the water? Become the flowing energy, the comfort, ease, and peace of the water element. Relax into the comforting essence of the water. Recognize the elemental qualities in yourself, and rest in them.

If you have been feeling ungrounded, open to the earth element. Go to the mountains, dig in your garden, or find another place where the earth energy is strong. Feel the stability, security, and connectedness of earth. You can take off your shoes and feel the solidity of earth beneath your bare feet, or sit or lie on the ground to allow your connection to deepen. If you have a mountain view, you can connect with the earth element by gazing with open awareness at the mountain. Wherever you are, allow a relationship with the earth element to form.

Open to the nourishment that earth offers you. To deepen your connection, you can communicate with the element and ask for its help. As you feel earth energy entering your body, receive this gift and rest. The fullness of connection may not happen right away, so give it time. At some point, you will feel the solidity of the earth element awaken within you. In this way you retrieve the essence of earth and heal your soul.

You can bring awareness to these sacred connections with the elements at any moment. If you tune in to the flow of nature and practice being in harmony with it, the natural elements will offer you more and more support. According to Bön teachings, there is a specific time of day that is most conducive to retrieving the support of each element. The space element is most powerful from midnight to 5 A.M. From 5 A.M. until 11 A.M., the fire element is most easily accessed. Between 11 A.M. and 4 P.M. is the best time for retrieving the water element. Air is most readily accessed between 4 P.M. and 9 P.M., and earth from 9 P.M. to midnight. These are the optimal times for retrieving the elements. But regardless of what time it is, if you meet an element fully with deep respect and gratitude, you will be rewarded.

Taking the Three Precious Pills

In order to receive the greatest benefit of the elements, you need to be fully present when you meet them in a natural setting. But as you seek connection with the spaciousness, liveliness, and warmth of the universe, you may encounter discomfort or mental chatter that interferes with a full connection. I refer to this discomfort as the pain body or pain identity—the ego-identity related to our physical, emotional, or mental pain. The pain body obscures the openness that is the source of all positive qualities. When your pain identity is active, the forest may be beautiful and the river may be inviting, yet you are unable to receive their gifts.

When you experience discomfort or distraction, bring your attention to the stillness of your body. As you continue to rest your focus there, your mind will begin to settle and you will be able to connect with a deeper sense of stillness. In this stillness, your pain identity releases, dissolving the boundary between you and the natural world around you. Feel the spaciousness of the sky above you, and with that support, find the spaciousness within you.

Listen and hear the silence within and around you. As you rest more fully in the silence, be aware of the openness you are experiencing.

Thoughts and distractions will most likely continue to arise in your mind. Recognize them, and host them without judging them. Embrace whatever arises in open awareness. As you do, your pain and distractedness will gradually dissipate, like clouds dispersing in the sky. Be aware of the natural warmth arising in each moment.

Stillness, silence, and spaciousness—the three precious pills—are medicine for your pain identity that you can take at any time. These qualities lead you to your inner wisdom, your natural mind—your true identity.

At the beginning of a retreat I once led, one of the participants was deeply troubled by conflicts he was having with his brother. I could tell that he was consumed by his thoughts and that more thinking would not help. He needed to free himself of his relentless pursuit of a solution. So I sent him into the woods with the other students, and instructed them to sit and just be with stillness, silence, and spaciousness. Over several days we quietly and peacefully watched the light filter through the trees. After one of these sessions, the student remarked that something had released. "I don't even remember what the problem was with my brother—it's gone!"

Opening Your Heart and Mind with Gratitude and Compassion

To experience the sacred in any relationship, it is necessary to open your heart and mind. You can begin by cultivating a feeling of gratitude toward nature. Do you appreciate the elements of nature and what they provide for you? As you take your morning shower, do you ever think, *I am so thankful for this warm water*? When you eat your midday meal, do you ever reflect on how much nourishment the earth has provided? Are you thankful for the sun's warmth that ripens the fruit, or for the air you breathe or the spaciousness of the sky? The more grateful you are, the more nourishment your soul will receive.

We are interdependent with the elements. We can live without a computer or a car, but we cannot live without earth, water, fire, air, and space. Gratitude for the elements can open and warm your heart.

You can open your heart further by developing compassion for the natural world. If you want a truly intimate relationship with your partner, your children, or others you love, you must be willing to put yourself in their place, to feel what they feel. This is also true of your relationship with nature.

Reflect on the suffering that animals, insects, and other beings of nature experience because of damage to their habitats. Nature programs on television expose the devastation that we humans have caused. By polluting the atmosphere, we have influenced a rise in global temperature, which in turn has contributed to an increase in natural disasters—droughts, floods, wildfires, and hurricanes. Many species have been displaced from their native habitats and face extinction because of overfishing, deforestation, oil spills, strip mining, and air and water pollution. Poultry and livestock suffer under inhumane conditions. To develop compassion, it's essential to not block awareness of the pain these beings suffer. Reflect on it. Feel it. Feeling deeply the pain of others, we develop a sincere wish that they be free of suffering.

Acknowledging our personal relationship to collective suffering is important. It is easy to feel powerless or complacent about the damage to nature that humans have caused. But each of us, as a member of the human race, is part of the problem. And this acknowledgment allows us to be part of the solution. The solution begins as we recognize our personal involvement, both direct and indirect, in the widespread destruction of nature.

In the Bön liturgy of soul retrieval, we confess our complicity in harming nature, express our sincere regret, and ask for forgiveness. Cultivating a genuine sense of regret is not the same as feeling guilt. Guilt is actually a block to transformation, but remorse can shift something deep within us and lead to positive action.

Some people, when contemplating their role in the destruction of our environment and the suffering that it causes, are overwhelmed by the immensity and complexity of the problem. Our willingness to face the implications of contributing to this suffering impels us to find solutions. If we are solution oriented, we can change many of our harmful behaviors. In a solution-oriented model, the amount of time spent dwelling on the wrongs we've done is short compared to the time we spend finding remedies. Once we see clearly and accept our part with regret, we can move forward.

What does moving forward look like? If you cultivate a genuine sense of regret and something shifts within you, then in time you will discover that you are spontaneously and effortlessly contributing to the solution through your individual and collective actions. It is important to develop a compassionate response to the suffering we perceive in the natural environment in order not to perpetuate harm. But while retrieving the elemental essences from the natural world, we also need to be fully conscious of nature's inherent beauty and completeness. As we open ourselves to the abundance of nature, we receive essential nourishment. Are you grateful for it?

Retrieving the Elemental Essences

Retrieving the elemental essences is like trying to remember something: if you try too hard, you can't remember. But when you stop trying, often what you have been searching for spontaneously comes to mind. So simply be still, silent, and open enough to allow positive qualities to emerge naturally. Cultivate an attitude of respect for the element and your relationship with it.

Each element of nature, whether earth, water, fire, air, or space, can support a powerful experience of transformation. After finding a place where the element you lack is abundant, open yourself to that element and connect with its healing qualities. Keep connecting. The longer you spend in relationship with the element, the more you will feel the essence of it coming alive in you.

As you deepen your relationship with the elements—with gratitude, compassion, and respect—your body, energy, and consciousness are fully engaged and awake. Through the sacred elements of the outer world, you discover the sacred elements within. Perhaps much of the loneliness experienced in modern culture is the result of being disconnected from the natural elements. Reigniting this sacred relationship brings you home to yourself and heals your soul.

The lively quality of nature will manifest as you quiet your mind. Give yourself time for this to take place. At first it might seem as if nothing is happening, but you will need to get past that perception or you will miss the relationship that is developing. It may take several dates with nature for the relationship to become a healing one. A mere glimpse of connection, while encouraging, is usually not enough for transformation.

There is a chance that even people who love nature—including those who make a living by managing natural resources or gardening, and those who support environmental issues and animal rights—may still lack a relationship with the natural world that is a bridge to inner wisdom. Someone may claim to enjoy gardening but see watering their plants as a chore, not as a sacred and joyful engagement. If you lack joy when interacting with nature, notice that lack and stop for a moment. Take one of the three precious pills—become aware of the stillness of your body, the silence of your speech, or the spaciousness of your mind, and enter into a deeper relationship with the natural world. Lack of joy is not your natural state, so wake up to the sacred relationship that is right in front of you. Nature is worthy of your attention.

As you engage the elemental energy and allow it to move within you, eventually you will feel it pervade your entire being. That's when you begin to dance with the element. Each of the elements can be fully engaged. As you dance with the element, your body comes alive with the quality you are seeking.

Opening to a Deeper Wisdom

In addition to bringing joy and balance into your life, connecting with nature and its elements supports you in developing spiritually. The soul-retrieval teachings of Bön have an inclusive perspective. There are many shamanic traditions that speak of the power of nature but do not necessarily guide you toward your wisdom qualities. There are Buddhist traditions that speak of wisdom but not of the power of nature. In my recent travels to Chile, I hiked in the mountains with some shamans who were vibrant in this natural setting. Then, when we returned to the teaching hall and I guided a meditation, they promptly fell asleep. Their experience of the external elements was very much alive, but their internal experience was not alive enough to keep them awake.

In Bön, soul-retrieval practices are considered stepping-stones on the path to enlightenment. Ultimately, nurturing a sacred relationship with the five elements of nature can lead to realization of the five wisdoms described in dzogchen, the highest teaching of Bön. When all five wisdoms are fully realized, one has attained the enlightened state.

The earth element is experienced as mirrorlike wisdom, or recognition of the clear, unobscured, and unchanging reflective quality of the nature of mind. Water is experienced as all-accomplishing wisdom, awareness that all phenomena are spontaneously, effortlessly, and naturally perfected. Fire is experienced as discriminating wisdom, the realization that every phenomenon is unique. Air is experienced as the wisdom of equanimity—the capacity to be grounded in even the most extreme situations by realizing the luminous innate awareness that is the base of all experience. Space is experienced as the wisdom of emptiness, the realization that all phenomena lack inherent existence.

When you gaze at the clear sky, it can support you in discovering the openness of your natural mind and can transmit a deep knowledge of the wisdom of emptiness. Each of the five elements is a doorway to wisdom. Each lends liveliness and richness to what might otherwise be a dry experience of contemplating the nature of mind. When the subtlest manifestations of the elemental energies, known as the five pure lights, are fully awakened in you, this is the ultimate healing for the soul.

Self-Guided Practice: Retrieving from Nature

Practical suggestions

Choose a safe location. Check the weather before going out in the elements. Bring whatever you need to be protected and comfortable: something to sit on (meditation cushion, folding chair, or blanket); food and water; layers of appropriate clothing; a hat; sunscreen. If you will be alone in a remote spot, let someone know where you are going and when you expect to return.

The posture you assume while practicing can affect the meditative experience. Sitting comfortably with legs crossed, spine straight, and chest open supports you by opening the flow of energy and guiding it through your body. If your physical condition does not permit such a posture, you can choose any sitting or lying position that is comfortable, open, and uplifting.

You can devote anywhere from half an hour to several hours to the practice. Continue to practice regularly until you experience signs of success in your daily life.

The Practice

Go into a natural setting where the element you need is particularly strong. Sit or lie comfortably and settle into your posture. Take a deep breath, hold it for a moment, and then exhale fully. Repeat several times. Then let your breath find a natural rhythm.

Bring your focus to the stillness of your body. Bring your focus to the silence of your speech. Bring your focus to the spaciousness of your mind. Allow stillness, silence, and spaciousness to quiet any restlessness, agitation, or distracting thoughts and bring you to a deeper state of peace. Rest in peacefulness.

Bring to mind the element you most need. Host any uncomfortable feelings or sensations you may be experiencing. Regard these feelings without judgment and with openness and warmth, as you would a friend in need. Feel how the lack of this element lives in your body, your emotions, and your mind. As you allow your thoughts and feelings, maintain a connection with stillness, silence, and spaciousness. Cultivate a sense of gratitude for the element you are retrieving and recognize how essential it is for your well-being.

Feel compassion for all beings, particularly those who are suffering because of the damage we humans have caused their natural environment. Acknowledge any role you have played. Feel deep regret for any harm you have caused, and ask for forgiveness.

Now reflect on the power and beauty of the element you are seeking, and how you would feel if this quality were restored to you. From stillness, silence, and spaciousness, open to the element and connect with its liveliness. Release any expectations, and open to whatever the element communicates to you. Be receptive.

If you feel moved, cultivate a physical relationship with the element. For example, lie on the earth, place your feet in the water, or open your arms wide to the wind. Be with the element. Feel its energy entering your body. As you breathe in, you can imagine you are inhaling directly into your heart the pure energy of the element. From your heart, feel the elemental energy expand to every cell of your body. As you breathe out, release any uncomfortable feeling or sense of lack. Each inhalation becomes medicine to enhance your life force and heal your soul. Each exhalation releases physical, energetic, and mental blockages.

Allow your body, energy, and consciousness to merge and move with the element. Let your experience be spontaneous and uncontrived.

Allow time to rest in whatever quality you have received. Just be.

At the conclusion of your session, bring to mind this intention: In liberating my own being, may I benefit others. As you dedicate your practice to the welfare of all beings, include in particular those who are suffering from the lack of the element you have retrieved.

ཡེ་ཤ་འདེ་།།བྱེ་།ཡ་ཡ་ཡེ་ཐ་པ་།།ཡེ་ཐ་པ་ཐུ་།ཟ།། །

ཐུན་འེ་།།བྱེ་།ཡ་ཡ་ཐུ་།ཨ་རྐུ་ཆེ་ཨ་པ་།ཟ།། །

འརེ་།འེ་།།བྱེ་།ཡ་ཡ་འརེ་།ཝ་རྐུ་ཆེ་ཨ་པ་།ཟ།། །

རེ་ཨ་འེ་།།བྱེ་།ཡ་ཡ་འཝ་ཙ་ཡ་ན་རེ་ཨ་ཆེ་ཨ་པ་།ཟ།། །

The mind and all mental states dissolve
into the space of the nature of mind.

All activities dissolve into the space of stillness.

All forms of speech dissolve into the space of silence.

All the clouds of thoughts and recollections
dissolve into the space free of thought.

—from *The Twenty-One Nails,*
a Bön dzogchen text

CHAPTER 3

Retrieving by Taking Inner Refuge

According to the dzogchen teachings, retrieving what was lost through communing with nature awakens something that already resides within you. Ultimately, there is no need to look outside yourself to heal the soul, for the true source of all the elemental essences is your inner refuge. At any given moment, connecting with this source gives you access to every quality you need for a healthy soul.

Perhaps you have noticed that, while sitting by a beautiful lake or walking on a mountain trail, you can access this inner refuge more easily. Such is the healing power of nature. And the reverse is also true. The more deeply you connect with the openness, awareness, and warmth of your authentic self, the more you will feel the healing qualities of the sacred elements reflected back to you from nature.

There are three aspects of inner refuge described in the dzogchen teachings. The way to access them is through the three doors: your body, speech, and mind.

The Refuge of Unbounded Sacred Space

You can access the first inner refuge, *unbounded sacred space,* through the stillness of your body.

Explore this now. Sit, close your eyes, and bring your attention to the stillness of your body. Take time to feel the stillness. As you rest in awareness of this simple and direct experience of stillness, your mind becomes calmer, quieter, and more settled and grounded.

Feeling the stillness and connecting deeply with it allows you to be fully present in the moment. Even in moments of restlessness, your physical agitation can remind you to draw your attention to stillness. Awareness of stillness can quiet your breathing and lower your heart rate, allowing anxiety to subside.

As you become more familiar with stillness and its grounding qualities, you experience just being. Stillness becomes a doorway to the first inner refuge: the unbounded sacred space of being. According to the dzogchen teachings in Bön and Tibetan Buddhism, unbounded sacred space is known as the *dharmakaya,* the body of emptiness. This is the changeless essence of your nature and the nature of all beings, and is the source of all the elemental essences. Major crises and other life challenges can create an imbalance of the elements, causing you to lose your energy and vitality, and with them, your soul. The antidote is to realize this changeless essence and take refuge in this unbounded sacred space. This brings you into balance and protects you from fear of change and loss. Connecting with this source allows the healing qualities of the elements to arise and manifest in you. Recognizing and abiding in this first refuge of unbounded sacred space heals your soul.

The Refuge of Infinite Awareness

Access to the second inner refuge, *infinite awareness*, is through the silence of your speech. Here, *infinite* refers to the limitless possibilities of each moment.

You can explore this now. Begin to listen to the silence within and around you. Refrain from talking, and as you become aware of your internal dialogue, draw your attention to the inner silence that is always present. Listen with your whole body. As you experience the silence, rest in it.

We have all wished for inner peace. Resting deeply in inner silence, you can experience it. Inner peace is natural to each of us. What separates us from peace is our smart ego, with its endless judgments, opinions, and advice. When you listen, hear, and rest in the inner silence, ego is allowed to rest, and you discover inner peace.

Still deeper within that inner peace is a sense of awareness—the second inner refuge. When your inner dialogue begins to release into silence, you become aware of the space of being. This awareness dawns like an inner light. It is traditionally referred to as the *sambhogakaya*, the body of light. It is the direct knowing of the unbounded sacred space of being. Through the light of awareness, you connect with your true nature. This brings a sense of richness, fullness, and worthiness, and heals your soul.

The Refuge of Genuine Warmth

The third inner refuge is *genuine warmth*. By *genuine* I mean authentic, not created by the ego. *Warmth* refers to a sense of bliss or well-being. Your doorway to this genuine warmth is through the spaciousness of your heart and mind.

Explore this now. Bring your focus to the space in and around your heart. Imagine it as a clear and open sky. As you connect internally with this sense of spaciousness, experience all the thoughts and images of your mind as moving within this sky. Rest in the spaciousness of the sky, open and aware.

At any given moment, when you are caught up in the stories and drama of your moving mind, you can bring your attention to the open sky of your mind. It is always there. Connect with it. Feeling and connecting deeply with this spaciousness brings an experience of genuine warmth. All that your soul needs to heal exists here in the warmth of being. In order to experience these healing qualities, you must connect with the openness and awareness of the first two refuges. From there, genuine warmth spontaneously arises.

The accommodating quality of the space element is naturally present. So is the flexibility of air, the inspiration of fire, the comfort of water, and the security of earth. So, too, are the four immeasurables: loving-kindness, compassion, joy, and equanimity. Traditionally, this third refuge is known as the *nirmanakaya,* the body of manifestation. Anytime you are conscious of needing a positive quality, you can find it here in the inner refuge. When you feel and share the warmth of the third refuge, your soul is nourished. You are whole.

The Wealth of the Inner Refuge

The three precious pills of stillness, silence, and spaciousness can help you connect with the true source of healing within. This connection may manifest as a subtle sense of comfort with who you are. When this connection is lively enough, it can bring deep feelings of love and compassion.

Should these positive feelings seem out of reach, look closer and you will see that you are not experiencing the first two refuges and therefore lack enough openness and awareness for these healing qualities to arise in you. It is as if your inner space is small and your problems are big.

If your pain identity is hosting another pain, the warmth of the positive healing qualities will not arise. You must be truly open. Holding your pain in open awareness without judging it or rejecting it allows the warmth to arise naturally from the openness of your being. Imagine a friend who comes to you in distress. How would your friend feel if you criticized her for feeling bad? But if instead you embraced her feelings from a place of openness, acceptance, and care, your friend's pain could ease naturally. Try hosting your own pain in the same way in the stillness, silence, and spaciousness with openness, acceptance, and caring attention.

Over time, by taking the three precious pills, you may be surprised by the warmth available to you in challenging situations. One of my students in a workshop wrote of such an experience:

> One of my biggest issues in life is noise. Noise gets to me, has made me sick at times. I even lived

in the middle of a forest for many years to avoid it, but noise can reach you anywhere, I've learned.

So I bought a nice house less than a year ago in a village and discovered this spring that it was extremely noisy. There are the sounds of constant traffic, lawnmowers, and my neighbor's machine shop. This neighbor really pushes my buttons.

One evening, as I was doing my meditation practice, I connected with the vast space inside. Moments later, my neighbor started up his chain saw only a few feet from the window in the room where I was practicing. Instead of feeling the usual high level of distress, I was unperturbed, even as a little voice whispered, *Come on, you hate the guy. This is horrible.* In addition, a big farm tractor rumbled by, and I felt it passing through me as simply a wave of energy.

When the noise stopped, I was overcome by a sense of unconditional love toward my neighbor. This came unannounced and surprised me. I can still feel it!

My student had been reacting to noise in anger because she lacked openness. Once she connected deeply with the space of inner refuge, she was able to perceive sound in its true nature—pure energy—and her negative emotions couldn't gain a foothold. In the space free of anger and aversion, the antidote—the genuine warmth of love—naturally arose.

Whatever your negative obstacles or feelings of lack, as you experience the openness of inner refuge, they will diminish, and the quality you need most will be free to manifest. This is what is meant by retrieving from the inner refuge.

The moment you take one of the three precious pills by bringing clear attention to stillness, silence, or spaciousness, you stop losing the elements of your soul. As you become more familiar with this process, at some point you feel genuine warmth. And as you become aware of the qualities associated with that warmth, you retrieve them.

Retrieving from the Inner Refuge

Personally, I find it energizing to look for the elemental essences in the challenges of everyday life. For example, in unsettling situations where we might think there is no stability at all, if I go into the space of inner refuge, I find that the stability and connectedness of the earth element are fully there. It becomes a question of trusting my ability to access them.

If you are feeling uncomfortable for no obvious reason, instead of searching for a reason, regard the discomfort as a lack of the water element. Look within and connect with unbounded sacred space, infinite awareness, and genuine warmth. As your pain and discomfort dissolve into the inner refuge, the ease, peacefulness, and fluidity of water naturally arise within you.

If the routine of your life lacks energy and enthusiasm, instead of changing your routine, look directly at this lack of fire. Close your eyes, go to the space of inner refuge, rest there, and trust that the qualities of the fire element are there. All the creativity, inspiration, and bliss you need are within.

When you are feeling stuck, in need of the flexibility of air, you have a choice. You can keep focusing on all your unresolved conflicts and unmet needs, or you can shift your attention instead to stillness, silence, and spaciousness. Connect with the inner refuge and trust that the air element will naturally become available.

We have a habit of dwelling on our problems. But when you feel anxious or preoccupied with a problem, consider talking less with your smart ego and turn instead to inner stillness, silence, and spaciousness. Come to the inner refuge and benefit from the riches within.

People who have lost their soul—who feel adrift, stressed out, separated from themselves—have lost connection to this quintessential experience of inner refuge that is our nature. They have lost the connection because their body, speech, and mind served as exit points. I encourage you to use these three doors as entryways, not exits. No matter where you go, you take your body, speech, and mind with you. At any given moment, entering through the stillness of your body, silence of your speech, and spaciousness of your heart and mind will help you find and connect with your authentic nature and the healing qualities within.

When you're in a rush and get stuck in traffic, how do you react? With many of us, our bodies tense up, our breathing gets shallow, anger or frustration flares, and the imagination goes wild: *Do you believe what those idiots are doing, blocking the intersection? Three green lights and we haven't moved.* If instead you use a traffic moment like that as a reminder to connect with stillness, silence, and spaciousness—and you do this often enough—over time even traffic will support a deep connection to yourself. The more connections you make between any challenge and the stillness, silence, and spaciousness of the inner refuge, the more you will be able to rely on the inner refuge and your ability to connect to it.

It's not just negative experiences that test us. Positive experiences in life can also be challenging. When we feel good, there is a natural tendency to want more of the good feeling and to want it to last. This is attachment, or grasping, an obstacle to abiding in the inner refuge. We can even become suspicious of feeling good: *Why am I feeling so good today? How long can this last?* As soon as our thoughts interfere in this way, the beauty of the moment is gone. But as we become more familiar with the inner refuge, we discover the ability to allow our experiences to be just as they are. A positive experience is not dependent on whether it lasts or not. So let your good moments, too, serve as a reminder to bring your attention to stillness, silence, and spaciousness.

With practice, the sense of fullness and completeness you can access through the inner refuge becomes your new normal. Another of my students wrote about the positive effect of connecting daily with unbounded space:

> After a while, without any evident reason, joy popped up from nowhere. Even though my life lately seems to be confronting me with great difficulties, I sometimes feel joy that seems to have no connection to what I'm dealing with at that moment. Even now I feel joy in writing to you about this. It sometimes feels as if I cannot hold back the exploding energy of that joy.
>
> There are beautiful changes in my everyday life: sudden appearances of peace or a love so strong that tears run down my cheeks, or a depth inside me I've never felt before—a longing to listen

to the silence inside when there is so much talking around me, to just listen and feel the protection.

Your Safest Haven

There is no better protection than the refuge of unbounded sacred space, infinite awareness, and genuine warmth. Any external source of refuge is ultimately unreliable. Looking for refuge in money or material possessions cannot protect you from the pain of loss, because everything you have will be lost to you someday. No matter how good your health insurance is or how healthy your lifestyle, sooner or later you will suffer from injury or sickness; eventually you will die. Finding your perfect soul mate cannot protect you from someday losing your beloved through separation, divorce, or death.

With the inner refuge, you are not depending on someone or something outside you to make you feel secure. The first refuge, unbounded sacred space, is a true support because it is unchanging, indestructible, beyond birth and death, eternal. Whatever difficulties you face, the first refuge supports you in allowing your experiences and hosting them fully. The second inner refuge, the light of awareness, can never be diminished or extinguished by any cause or condition. Inner light is unceasing—forever luminous and clear. Even in the darkest of circumstances, you can trust that it is always there. You can also trust that the warmth of the third refuge is within you. It spontaneously arises from the union of openness and awareness.

There may be moments when you feel emotionally cold and dark, when it seems that all the light has gone from your life. But your experience and inner truth are not in sync—the light is always there. At these moments, access to the inner refuge may seem distant, but a sense of trust may bring you a glimmer of the inner refuge that can lead to a shift in the darkness of your experience. Trust is a necessary companion on the path. There is no situation so bad that you can't turn toward the three doors. As you become more familiar with entering and abiding in the inner refuge, you will begin to trust in its healing presence.

We all long for that inner connection, just as a lost child longs to reunite with his or her mother. When you connect with the inner refuge, you can rest in that space just as a child rests in his or her mother's loving arms, feeling protected, safe, secure, complete.

Beyond the Ego

There is a Tibetan joke about a yogi who leaves his hermitage to get supplies. Afraid of getting lost in a crowded marketplace, he ties a red ribbon around his leg. As long as the ribbon is there, he feels secure. But at one point he looks down and notices that the ribbon has fallen off. He frantically runs back and forth through the market, yelling, "I'm lost! I'm lost! Did anyone see me? I'm the one wearing the red ribbon around his leg."

His reaction may seem quite silly to us, but most of us react in a similar way. We lose our job, or an important relationship comes to an end, and we feel lost. *Who am I?* We forget where we put our cell phone, and we panic and feel disoriented. *Where am I?* We have all experienced losing the red ribbon. But the truth is, we are never lost.

Drawing attention to stillness, silence, and spaciousness shifts your focus from feeding the insecurity of the ego to connecting with pure being. Anytime you identify with a sense of "I"—"I feel something"; "I have lost something"; "I am lost"—you are identifying with the wrong person. You are identifying with the ego, with your pain body, not with your true nature.

Being aware of the three doors is not work. In fact, the more effort you put into connecting with stillness, silence, and spaciousness, the more elusive the inner refuge seems. Connecting with the inner refuge is simply a matter of shifting your attention. If you are already still, be aware of stillness. When you are silent, hear the silence that is already there. Notice the spaciousness at the very center of your being. As you rest in awareness, you connect with your authentic self. The effort of seeking dissipates, and you *are* unbounded sacred space, infinite awareness, and genuine warmth—you *are* the inner refuge. The inner sacred space is so simple and close that if we search for it, we cannot find it. But it is always there for you, the source of all the elemental qualities you need. As the inner refuge, you are whole and complete in each moment.

Self-Guided Meditations: Retrieving from the Inner Refuge

Formal Practice

I recommend setting aside at least 30 minutes each day to sit quietly in meditation.

To begin, sit comfortably with legs crossed, spine straight, and chest open. If your physical condition does not permit such a posture, choose any upright position that is comfortable, open, and uplifting. Settle into your posture. Take a deep breath, hold it for a moment, and then exhale fully. Repeat several times. Then let your breath find a natural rhythm. Reflect on the element you need most at this time.

The first inner refuge:

Gradually bring your attention inward. Be aware of the stillness of your body from the crown of your head to the soles of your feet. Give your physical body loving attention. As your body rests in the warmth of awareness, every cell responds. Feel a sense of well-being from this caring attention.

Rest in stillness. If your mind wanders, gently bring it back. It is one thing to be physically still, another thing to be aware of that stillness. When you are aware of stillness, it will support you.

Through the doorway of stillness, gradually become aware of simply being open. This is a glimpse of the unbounded sacred space of the inner refuge. Trust this.

Rest in that refuge for as long as the experience remains fresh.

The second inner refuge:

Listen and hear the silence in and around you. Listen with your entire body. Feel the silence throughout your whole being.

Gradually, through the door of silence, allow yourself to experience a deep sense of peace. As you rest here, awareness of unbounded space dawns, fresh, clear, and lively, and you connect with authentic presence.

Rest here as long as the experience remains fresh.

The third inner refuge:

Draw clear and open attention to your heart. Be aware of the spaciousness at the center of your being. This space is like a clear, open sky.

You are that sky. Be aware of it, feel it, connect with it.

When the sky is clear, the sun shines and you feel its warmth. Allow a sense of warmth to arise within you. Feel and connect with that genuine warmth.

Appreciate this and rest here as long as the experience remains fresh.

Retrieving the element:

In this inner refuge of unbounded sacred space, infinite awareness, and genuine warmth, reflect on the loss of your soul or vitality in your personal life, in your family and close relationships, and in your professional life. Notice any sense of lack. Recognize this lack without judging, criticizing, or getting caught up in stories. Just be aware and host your experience in the warmth of inner refuge.

If you lack the security of the earth element, host the feeling of insecurity. If you lack the comfort of water, host your discomfort. If you lack the inspiration of fire, the flexibility of air, or the openness of space, host those feelings.

Host your experience as the sky hosts the clouds, allowing whatever arises to come, stay, and go.

As you connect deeply with the inner refuge, your experience of lack releases. Be aware of the openness that remains. Imagine the joy a lost child feels when reunited with his or her mother. Allow the same sense of joy as you recognize your own inner mother, your authentic self, the truth of who you are. With this recognition, your heart opens. Feel that you are receiving love, attention, and protection.

Whatever elemental qualities you are missing are available in this moment.

If earth is what you need, the essence of earth is here. In this sacred space is a sense of groundedness, of connectedness. By drawing your attention inward, you find the nourishment of earth. As you open to earth's qualities, you retrieve them.

If you need the water element, the essence of water is here. When you are aware of the inner refuge, you find a natural sense of comfort—the comfort of being as you are. In that moment you are freed from what you have been trying to become. You are complete. That sense of completeness and comfort is the water element. As you open to water's qualities, you retrieve them.

If you are in need of fire, the essence of fire is here. When you connect deeply with stillness, silence, and spaciousness, you discover qualities associated with fire—creativity, energy, inspiration, enthusiasm. As you open, connect, and feel the warmth of fire's qualities, you retrieve them.

If air is what you lack, the essence of air is here in the inner refuge. Connect to the source within to find the playfulness, curiosity, and flexibility that are qualities of the air element. As you bring your attention to the dynamic qualities of air and become familiar with them, you retrieve them.

If you are disconnected from the benefits of the space element, space is here. The very nature of inner refuge is spaciousness. The space element accommodates all of existence, including every experience you perceive. To retrieve space, be aware of that sense of openness and accommodation. Connect deeply with it. In this way, you retrieve the space element, and it will support you.

Continue to rest in the gifts of the inner refuge. Trust completely in what is available here. Allow your soul to be nourished by the elemental qualities you longed for and have now retrieved.

As you rest even more deeply, any sense of separation releases, and you discover that you *are* the unbounded sacred space, infinite awareness, and genuine warmth.

Rest in this experience for as long as it remains fresh.

To dedicate the merit of your practice, bring to mind this intention: *In liberating my own being, may I benefit others.*

Informal Practice

Anytime you face a challenge at work, in relationships, or in your time alone, when you start to feel anxious, agitated, or irritated, recognize where you are focusing your attention. Much of the time we focus on the people, circumstances, or tasks that bother us, and engage in an inner dialogue about them. Instead, take a moment or two and shift your attention inward to stillness, silence, and spaciousness.

Trust the space that opens up within you. Take refuge through stillness, silence, and spaciousness. This can immediately change your experience of what is happening within and around you. Everything you need at a particular moment arises from the inner refuge. Commit to connecting with the inner refuge as often as possible throughout your day.

This practice is also beneficial when positive feelings arise. Whenever you experience love, joy, happiness, contentment, or some other warm quality, let those moments remind you to bring awareness to the stillness of your body, silence of your speech, and spaciousness of your mind. Rest in the warmth of the inner refuge.

Staying with these experiences as long as they are fresh protects and nourishes you. It protects you from losing connection with the inner refuge and allows you to experience yourself as a warm and loving being.

Through the repeated informal practice of taking the three precious pills, whatever interactions you engage in or emotions you experience can be hosted in unbounded sacred space, infinite awareness, and genuine warmth, the qualities of the inner refuge. This is the ultimate protection from soul loss.

ཉེ། །ཡང་ངེ། །ཡ་ཛེ། །ཡ་ཁ་རྒྱ་པ་ཀེ། །ཡེ་པ་ཀྱེ་ག །

སྐ། །ག། །ག། །ཛེ་ན་ར། །ག། །ག་ནཚེ་ར། །ཁྱེ་ནརྒྱ་ས། །

ར། །ཡ་ག་ནག་ག། །ཡ་ཛེ། །ཡེ་ཡ་པ་རྷ་ག་ཀེ། །ཡེ་པ་ཀྱུ་ཡ། །

སྐ། །ཡེ་རྗེ་པ་ཀྱེ། །ཡ་ནག། །ག་ནཚུ་ཡ་པ་ཁྱ་པ། །

Seeing yourself as you are,
you attain buddhahood and are freed.

Obtaining power over appearances,
you have the mastery of a world conqueror.

Seeing self as other, sentient beings are deluded.

Chasing after appearances,
you become enchanted and deceived
by these illusions.

—from *The Twenty-One Nails,*
a Bön dzogchen text

CHAPTER 4

Retrieving from Relationships

Small children look cute and lovable when they are napping. Watching them, you feel warm inside. As you observe them being still, silent, and spacious, they help you experience and embrace those same qualities.

Of course, once your child wakes up and starts jumping around, screaming, and creating chaos, you may feel like screaming and acting crazy in return. In those moments you may think that the child has stolen all your stillness, silence, and spaciousness. In any relationship, when things are stressful and you are caught in a pattern of reactivity or negative emotion, you may feel drained of your vitality. But the very moment of chaos in a relationship can be a doorway to the inner refuge.

Through any external appearance—any form, event, or relationship—you can either become separate from yourself or connect with the richness of the inner refuge and the elemental qualities you need. If two people have a deep connection with each other, that connection, however wonderful, is not the refuge itself. No matter how deep our love for another is, it is accompanied by wants, needs, and hopes, and therefore by disappointments or suffering. But in taking the three precious pills in moments of either bliss or challenge, bringing full awareness to the stillness of the body, silence of speech, and spaciousness of mind, you enter the inner refuge.

When your child is throwing a tantrum, look within. Take the three precious pills, and you will discover that your inner resources have *not* been stolen from you. What's more, if you can feel the stillness underlying your child's wild actions and the silence behind the screaming, your child might feel those same qualities and begin to calm down. As you embody the same qualities you saw in your sleeping child, your warm presence becomes available to your child.

Resting in the inner refuge not only protects us from being drained by others but also allows us to support them. Opening our heart to others helps us feel positive qualities such as compassion and joy. By coming back to our true nature in relationships, we heal our soul.

Showing, Not Telling

Many of us have a deep desire to help others. Parents often ask me how they can teach meditation to their children. I've learned from experience that whenever I try to explain something to my nine-year-old, he is not particularly interested. It works far better to show than to tell. I used to get up very early to do my morning meditation practice, but now I practice after my son wakes up. He loves to sit nearby, watch me, and listen to the Tibetan chants I play as I'm doing prostrations. Sometimes when I am in mid-prostration he jumps onto my back. That makes it hard for me to stand up again, but I don't see it as a disturbance—I look at it as an opportunity to teach him prostrations. He is observing me, listening to me, connecting with me. One day he exclaimed, "I love this chanting!" He is hearing and feeling the prayers, but no one is making him listen to them. Learning can happen spontaneously when we simply allow connection—even while someone is jumping on us!

I sometimes experiment with sharing my connection to the inner refuge with my son. In the moment of entering into stillness, silence, and spaciousness, I feel warmth and bring light and warmth to my eyes so that he can receive that light and warmth from me. I'm not telling him to do anything or asking anything of him. As I look at him, I offer him a simple expression of joy and love. He responds with a brief smile. I repeat this exercise throughout the day. In this way I offer my son an opportunity to experience the beauty of the essence of who he is in the moment. As I allow him to experience who he is, I feel an even greater sense of who I am. In these moments of connection, soul healing takes place.

Unexpected Connections

Our reactive pain identity disconnects us from our genuine warmth and filters our experience of the world around us, including our relationships with loved ones. Often we project our distress onto people around us, particularly those we are closest to, thinking that it is their behavior and not our own discontent that is the source of our unhappiness. Connecting with stillness gives you a break from your pain body. Being aware of silence gives you a break from your pain speech. Connecting with the spaciousness of mind and the resulting warmth gives you a break from your negative imagination. In this freedom from your own pain, however brief, you can hear your partner clearly and empathize with his or her pain. Feeling supported by the inner refuge, you connect more openly, and true healing can take place.

If you look at a loved one from a place of anger, you will always see justification for your anger. But when you view the person from the place of stillness, silence, and spaciousness, you are likely to see someone who is hurting and may need your love, care, and compassion. By remaining open and available to the other person, you are permitting a genuine connection to happen. Instead of exchanging angry words, you may find yourselves expressing tenderness toward each other.

One of my students wrote about how she prepared in advance for a difficult conversation with a friend. She explained that her dear friend had a way of constantly engaging in pain-related speech that drained everyone around her. My student wanted to stay clear and connected during the conversation, so she did a simple breathing practice beforehand to release any negativity she was feeling and connect with the spaciousness within herself. Later, she described what happened:

> My mind felt clear, sharp, and awake. In this state, I listened to my friend without agreeing or disagreeing. She went on for a few rounds, and her tone of speech gradually turned from frantic to surprisingly self-aware. At one point, the setbacks and problems that were very real for her were demoted in her mind to what she called "stories told repeatedly." It amazed me that my own internal

transformation might have affected my friend's pain speech.

Nurturing the Elemental Qualities

Before you can share your inner refuge with others, you must become familiar with it on your own and embody it. Familiarity takes practice. Try making a daily routine of the formal meditation practice, Retrieving from the Inner Refuge, in Chapter 3. And informally, at any given moment of your day, remember to connect with the three precious pills. Whenever possible, recognize and rest in the unbounded sacred space, infinite awareness, and genuine warmth of the inner refuge.

When you feel the warmth of elemental qualities arising in you—the qualities you most need at that time—be aware of those feelings and allow them fully. Whether you are feeling a sense of comfort, security, inspiration, or playfulness, give your full attention to that emerging quality, just as you would to a dear friend after a long separation. Even if you had other things planned that day, you would rearrange your schedule to be with that loved one.

I want to emphasize the importance of noticing and fully experiencing the positive quality when it arises. We often neglect to do this in our meditation practice, much less in our daily lives. We rush through our experience without nurturing it. I talk more about this in Chapter 6, Nourishing Your Inner Being. The essential point is that for every moment you fully experience an elemental quality, you nourish your soul. This needs to be appreciated.

Sharing the Elemental Qualities

As with the gifts of openness and awareness, in order to share the gift of genuine warmth, you need to feel it in yourself. Just as when you are anxious and others may sense it no matter how hard you try to hide it, when you feel grounded, others feel warm and secure in your presence. When you feel at ease, people tend to feel at ease around you. When you feel a creative spark, others are energized. When you feel flexible, others can enjoy a sense of freedom. When you feel spacious, those who spend time with you are likely to feel more open and accommodating.

There is no better gift you can give than the warmth of your open heart. There's a story in my tradition that illustrates the full power of this warmth.

Once there was an accomplished meditation master who sensed that he was nearing the end of his life. He was feeling free and open, connected to all those around him, and ready to die. But his attendant was anxious and reminded the master that he needed to put his affairs in order. How did he intend to distribute his possessions and delegate his responsibilities? The conversation forced the master to think about worldly affairs, and this agitated him so much that upon his death, he became a disturbing ghost.

This ghost was very possessive. For weeks after the master's death, his ghost haunted anyone who even touched his things. Lamas were called in to try to liberate him from suffering and free everyone else from his torments, but the ghost was so powerful that he disrupted the lamas' practices and rituals.

Then a simple monk arrived who tried to pacify the ghost using a practice of tantric visualization, in which he manifested as a powerful deity. But instead of being pacified, the ghost transformed into an even more powerful tantric deity. Seeing this display, the monk realized that although the ghost had great power, he still lacked warmth. The monk wept. *How sad,* he thought, *that such a dedicated practitioner has come to this.* The monk's compassion so moved the ghost that he was able to listen, finally, to the monk's teachings.

You can regularly rest in the inner refuge, retrieve the element you need, nourish yourself with it, share it with others, and still not notice immediate changes in yourself or the people around you. You might not immediately tame all your ghosts. But each time you host your own pain or another's pain in openness, awareness, and warmth, the pain transforms and the strength of the pain identity is weakened. Enlightenment is a long journey. Never give up.

Giving Space to Suffering

Everyone heals and grows in his or her own time. It's important to be open to your own and others' suffering and imperfections, and not to expect that healing will follow a prescribed schedule.

When someone you love is hurting, of course you want to do anything you can to ease his or her pain. Sometimes, however, pain may be necessary for our growth and evolution. For example, people with addictions often need to feel deeply the pain that their harmful habits bring to themselves and their loved ones before they can relinquish those habits. People who have lost a loved one need to go through a grieving process in order to accept their loss and reengage life fully.

In an ideal world there would be no pain. Real life, though, is filled not only with joy and humor but also with suffering and sadness. We need to give space to our own and others' afflictions. Consider that one day you will be facing death, and the only way to die in peace will be to accept the reality of your situation. By openly accepting your loved ones' suffering, you can contribute to their sense of peace and be a comfort to them.

In some situations, it can be especially difficult to accept another person's pain—for example, when the person refuses to take action that could help them feel better. Your father with lung disease won't stop smoking cigarettes. Your sister who is depressed keeps drinking too much alcohol. Your best friend who's in an abusive relationship won't leave the abuser or seek help. When you watch someone suffer in this way, it's easy to feel angry, disappointed, sad, or helpless. But if anger or helplessness is all you have to give, that's not very supportive. Consider taking a short break from the problem. Go for a walk and come back later when you are feeling more spacious. Taking time to renew yourself is far better than stewing in frustration.

Often when we're in the presence of someone who is suffering, we join in the suffering, thinking that we are connecting with the person. A kinder and wiser approach would be to take the three precious pills and rest in the inner refuge. There, you are empowered to share the healing gift of genuine compassion, and the other person can benefit from your presence.

When Emotions Are Difficult

People push our buttons. Your partner points out your faults; your boss criticizes your work; your good friend takes sides against you. When you are the one in the relationship who is hurting, what do you do? Instead of looking to the other to make you feel better, look inward toward the inner refuge. Sometimes feeling better is just a matter of shifting your focus. As soon as you begin to feel distress in your body, draw your attention to the stillness of your body. As soon as your thoughts or words take you away from yourself, listen to the silence behind your speech. As soon as your mind starts jumping from one imaginary scenario to the next, bring your awareness to your heart and find the spaciousness there. If you can still your pain body, silence your pain speech, and focus your mind in the right way, your distress will dissipate and you will connect with your inherent worthiness.

A student wrote about how her practice supported her during a stressful encounter:

> Yesterday I had occasion to interact with a person with whom I have had many difficulties. As I was talking to this person, I was using awareness of my breath to create space around my familiar feelings of frustration and annoyance. I came to the realization that the problem was not that this person was annoying and frustrating me; rather, it was my narrow perception of this person that caused me to react with impatience. Once I put space around my feelings, my entire view of this person changed. I saw them in a completely different light, as someone who is suffering just like me. My heart and mind opened to them, and I could

palpably sense a shift in our relationship. It was such a rewarding experience!

Here in the West, I've noticed that many people try to resolve conflicts by expressing their negative emotions outwardly rather than by bringing awareness inward to their spacious natures. For example, when a couple is in conflict, the husband may speak from a place of anger and the wife from a place of fear. They are two beautiful human beings with good intentions, but in their anger and fear they confront and argue with each other. Expressing negative emotions does not resolve the problem: it *is* the problem. What comes from disconnectedness cannot create connectedness.

By the time you are angry or upset with someone, it can be difficult to find the space and light in your emotions, much less feel genuine warmth. If you get caught up in emotion and say or do something destructive, at the very least try to be aware of your transgression. Without awareness of your negative attitudes and actions, you are far more likely to keep on engaging in conflict. And the more often you engage, the more concrete and external-ized your problems may seem: "What she did to me was terrible!" "He's the one with the problem!" When you see the problem as outside of you, you are disinclined to work on yourself. You will be more inclined to justify your ac-tions, blame the other person, or just put the whole thing out of mind.

So at the very least, reflect on your behavior and rec-ognize that you can bring your tendency to react into your daily practice. In your practice you can loosen the appar-ent solidity of any situation. Through regular practice, you can engage all your relationships and social interactions from the inner refuge, and they become a source of nourishment rather than a source of dissatisfaction.

Dissolving the Pain Identity

Through regular practice, you may also find that you are less driven by your ego. The ultimate goal of meditation practice and soul retrieval is to relinquish the false self—the pain identity—and recognize the truth of being fully awake in every moment.

How do we recognize and relinquish the false self, the ego? We need to become sensitive to our painful reactions to others and bring our attention to them. When we bring clear and open attention, free of judgment, to our reactions, we become aware of the pain identity. As we host this pain identity and embrace it with open awareness, it dissolves, because we are no longer feeding it with our judgments and pain imagination.

But what happens if you don't recognize this pain identity? When interpersonal conflicts arise, pain imagination projects onto others. You may assume they are not listening to you or are trying to annoy you. You may expect them to notice your pain, while you fail to acknowledge theirs.

Out of fear and anxiety we tend to assign negative qualities to other people. But focusing on the negative can drain you and harm your relationships. If you keep dwelling on the fact that your partner or teenage child always leaves dishes in the sink, you will continually feel depleted. But the cause of the suffering is not the dirty dishes in the sink but your assumption that your partner or teenager is ignoring the dishes just to annoy you. Your pain identity has spun a tale that leaves you feeling like a victim. When this pain identity dissolves, you experience openness, awareness, and warmth, and are more likely to appreciate positive qualities in other people. Instead of fretting about the dishes, you may be able to simply enjoy an affectionate exchange with your partner or child. Recognizing positive qualities has a healing effect on your soul and benefits those around you.

Self-Guided Practices: Retrieving from Relationships

Formal Meditation Practice

If you've been practicing Retrieving from the Inner Refuge from Chapter 3 once a day for 30 minutes, I recommend that you now do two 30-minute meditation sessions a day, ideally at the beginning and end of the day. You may also wish to practice Retrieving from the Inner Refuge not only for yourself but also for a friend or loved one who is sick, in pain, or otherwise in need of soul retrieval.

Practicing for Another Person:

As you connect deeply with stillness, silence, and spaciousness, and rest in unbounded sacred space, infinite awareness, and genuine warmth, imagine that the other person is with you now.

As you host your own pain in the space of inner refuge, feel that you are hosting the other person's pain as well.

As you retrieve the elemental qualities, imagine and feel that your friend or loved one is also receiving those qualities. Experience vividly that the other person, like you, is connecting deeply with these qualities and being healed.

Bring to mind this intention: *In liberating my own being, may I benefit others.* As you dedicate your practice to the welfare of all beings, include your friend or loved one in the dedication.

Informal Meditation Practice

The more familiar you are with bringing your attention to the three doors of stillness, silence, and spaciousness, abiding in the inner refuge during formal meditation, the more easily you will remember to access these three precious pills during day-to-day interactions with family, friends, and colleagues. You can take the three precious pills anytime you are about to engage with another person at work, at home, or elsewhere. Try to practice informally at least five times every day.

Instead of anticipating a meeting with someone by thinking about what you'll say or how you'll act, let such moments remind you to first bring your attention to stillness, silence, and spaciousness. Become aware of any expectations you might be holding and allow them to release. Host yourself and the other person in the open space of inner refuge. Allow your interaction to take place from that space.

You can engage in the informal practice in three different situations: supportive, neutral, and challenging.

Supportive situations: These include any social engagement in which you exercise love, generosity, compassion, openness, or other positive qualities. For example, you might be serving others by working in your spiritual community or volunteering in a soup kitchen. Use these moments as an opportunity to feel and cultivate the positive elemental qualities that naturally arise from the space of inner refuge.

Neutral situations: Once you are having good experiences as you practice in supportive settings, explore accessing the inner refuge and the elemental qualities in neutral situations, such as while grocery shopping, running errands, doing household chores, or preparing a meal.

Challenging situations: As you feel more connected to the inner refuge in neutral settings, you can use less comfortable engagements as reminders to turn within. Challenging situations might include having difficult conversations, managing health issues, moving, losing a job, seeking employment, or grieving the death of a loved one.

Neutral and challenging situations are instances in which you normally lose connection with yourself. But with the right awareness, these, too, can be opportunities to access a deeper source within.

ཞེ་ཡ་བདྲི་ཤེས་ཆེ་ཡུ་ཁ་ཕྱེ་ཕེ་ཕྱུ་ར་ཁ་རྫོགས།།

Because the door to the treasure
of the mind is opened,

Everything you need is complete within you.

—from *The Twenty-One Nails,*
a Bön dzogchen text

CHAPTER 5

Overcoming
Loneliness

Students often ask me for advice on overcoming feelings of isolation and loneliness. Being around people is not necessarily the antidote. I feel this topic merits special consideration, as there is a strong relationship between loneliness and soul loss.

Today, millions of people around the world are connected virtually, yet many seem to be more disconnected than ever emotionally and spiritually. We can be living with hundreds of people in the same building, using the same elevator, walking the same streets, eating in the same neighborhood restaurants, communicating on the same social networks, and still feel a sense of disconnection.

Retrieving your soul starts with finding a deeper connection within. From there, a deeper connection with others is possible. If you can engage skillfully in the practices in this book—including the one at the end of this chapter—it is unlikely that loneliness will remain an issue for you, even if you live alone. When your soul is healed— when all the elements come into balance and you feel whole and connected within yourself—you no longer look to others to make you feel complete.

When Loneliness Arises

Loneliness is part of being human. But for many people, it is a chronic and unwelcome companion. You could spend all day with your partner and sleep next to him every night and still feel lonely. Loneliness brings a deep sense of longing for someone or something to fill your need for connection. You may feel lost or left out, without joy, enthusiasm, or motivation. Not only does loneliness deplete your soul but it can also harm your health. It has been linked to a variety of undesirable conditions, including depression, increased blood pressure, sleep problems, a weakened immune system, and decreased mental cognition in the elderly.[1]

Some people react to loneliness by dwelling on their dark feelings. Others distract themselves with activities like shopping, cleaning, organizing, and surfing the Web. In the West many people engage in a lot of activity not because they are inspired by what they are doing but because they feel social pressure to stay busy. Staying busy is not seen as a virtue in the Tibetan culture. Certainly, if you want to keep busy, you can do so, but don't anticipate an internal awakening as a result!

Conventional wisdom tells us that the best antidote to loneliness is a relationship or an active social life. It's true that human contact can serve as a temporary relief from the pain of loneliness, but once you're in a relationship, is it truly intimate and connected? You can't be intimate with someone else unless you're intimate with yourself. You can't be happy with someone else if you're not happy with yourself. You can't connect with someone else if you're not connected with yourself. The true medicine for loneliness is the connection with the inner refuge. It's about feeling at home with yourself.

Many people who feel lonely and engage in social activity continue to feel chronically dissatisfied with where they are, who they are with, and what they are doing. A man may be sitting with his wife in silence in a restaurant and feel little inspiration to connect with her, yet he may have a strong desire to connect with the people having a lively conversation at the next table. Someone with a great job may lack interest in her own work but be obsessed with how appealing her co-worker's job seems to be.

If you lack intimacy in your personal life and you continually look elsewhere for a sense of connection, you are unlikely to find what you are seeking. This pattern of looking elsewhere for satisfaction misses the point of where true connection lies.

Finding the Friend Within

A sense of loneliness may be triggered by the loss of someone close to you, through the breakup of a friendship or marriage, perhaps, or the death of a loved one. It may arise when someone you care about seems to be unable to make time for you. People who suffered abuse or neglect in childhood often find it difficult to connect meaningfully with others. While the absence or loss of a positive relationship can trigger loneliness, the true cause of loneliness is within—disconnection from yourself. When you have not connected with yourself fully, you do not feel complete. You lack the nourishment of the essential qualities—the stability of earth, the comfort of water, the enthusiasm of fire, the free-flowing movement of air, the openness of space.

I had a conversation with a husband and wife who had attended a workshop I had just given. They had been in conflict over the wife's frequent trips to visit her sister. While the visits filled the wife with joy, her husband felt left out, so he frequently asked her to stay home with him instead of going away as often as she did. The husband explained that during the workshop he had come to understand the value of feeling open and giving space to others. He had been feeling closed, lonely, and jealous each time his wife left and wanted her to stay home in order to relieve his loneliness and jealousy. But that kind of relief, he now realized, would reinforce an unhealthy experience of himself as a jealous person. Instead of focusing on his loneliness, he could now discover the openness within himself and the beauty of seeing his wife go on a trip that clearly meant so much to her. He told me that now he was excited about buying his wife a plane ticket to visit her sister. "Her freedom is my freedom; her joy is my joy," he said.

A primary method for overcoming loneliness is to retrieve your soul, whether from nature, the inner refuge, or relationships. Finding the Friend Within, the self-guided practice at the end of this chapter, is based on the practice of inner refuge you have been doing, but in this case loneliness and the loss of connection provide the doorway to connecting with your essential nature.

Before engaging in this practice, it is important to have compassion for yourself, just as you would for others who feel lonely. A typical response to loneliness would be to avoid looking at our feelings, to reject or judge the feelings or ourselves for being lonely, or to remain stuck in our misery. But in this meditation you are doing for yourself what you would do for a friend who feels lonely. As you become conscious of your negative feelings, you will be guided to host them, offering them your company and friendship.

Before you begin the practice, I recommend taking a few minutes to reflect on the specific connection you are missing that makes you feel lonely. For example, did you lose an important person in your life—someone who seemed to take all your happiness and inspiration with him when he left? Did you lose a valued connection with someone who brought out the best in you, or who supported or guided you in difficult times? Or have you been looking for someone to fill your need for connection?

In this practice you are encouraged to bring this lack or loss into your awareness and to fully allow any associated sense of pain, sadness, or loneliness. You will be hosting your feelings in stillness, silence, and spaciousness, in the inner refuge. You will be giving a spacious, luminous, warm hug to your pain. As you host your feelings of loneliness in the warmth of your genuine presence, they begin to transform.

Some people spend the better part of their lives trying to find a soul mate, achieve recognition or status, or accumulate wealth. They do so in order to not feel lonely and to feel more worthy and complete. But the satisfaction you achieve from external sources is fleeting by nature. Even if you were to restore the very relationship you have been missing so deeply and for so long, your loneliness would not necessarily be resolved. Finding yourself through the inner refuge is the most powerful medicine for overcoming loneliness and achieving a lasting sense of fullness and completeness.

Self-Guided Practice: Finding the Friend Within

Formal Practice

Engage in this practice for at least 20 to 30 minutes a day, working with the loss or lack of relationship until you notice that your feelings of loneliness have lessened.

Sit comfortably, with your spine straight and chest open. Bring your attention inward.

Take a few deep breaths. Use each exhalation to release whatever tension you are holding in your body, your breath, and your mind.

Completely let go of all thoughts and experiences by bringing your focus to your body. Since in this moment your body is already still, be aware of that stillness and connect with it. Each moment of connection helps your mind to calm and rest. If you lose the connection to stillness in your body, your mind will no longer be supported and will wander. Simply reconnect and continue resting in that stillness.

Gradually bring your attention to the silence of your speech. Be aware of it. Listen, hear, feel, and connect with the inner silence. Feel its beauty and peacefulness. If you lose awareness of the silence and you no longer hear it, or you are listening to inner chatter instead, simply reconnect to the silence and rest in it.

Now bring your attention to your heart and be aware of the spaciousness around and within it. Feel the power and blessings of this openness. If you lose this connection, be aware that you have lost it. Reconnect and continue resting in that sacred space.

All three doors—the stillness of the body, the silence of speech, and the spaciousness of the mind—lead to the unbounded inner sacred space, the source of everything. This space is primordially pure and perfected, with the potential to manifest all qualities, including those of the elemental essences and the four immeasurables: love, compassion, joy, and equanimity. Be aware of that space and rest in it, as a baby rests in the loving arms of its mother. You are that baby, and the mother space is the trustworthy source of all nourishment. Resting there, you feel loved and acknowledged, warm and connected. As you rest in the mother space, merge with the space and become the loving mother.

Now bring into awareness the personal connection you have been missing. As you feel your sense of lack or loss fully, host that sense of loneliness in the unbounded sacred space. As you host it, loneliness begins to disperse. Allow time for this to happen. Trust the space.

When you glimpse even a little sunshine between the clouds in the sky within you, experience this space and light. Connect with the experience. It is always there for you, as your friend and support.

As the sense of connection deepens, recognize that you are connecting with your fundamental nature, with who you truly are.

Rest in this experience for as long as it remains fresh.

Dedicate your practice to all beings, particularly those who are suffering from loneliness, with this intention: *In liberating my own being, may I benefit others.*

Informal Practice

Throughout your day, be conscious of those moments when you feel lonely. Let that feeling remind you to shift your attention to the stillness of your body, the silence of your speech, and the spaciousness of your mind. Just as sunshine gradually disperses the morning mist to reveal the clear, blue sky, the light of your awareness will gradually dissolve the loneliness. Rest in the clear sky of your being as you would rest with a best friend.

Repeat this informal practice at least five times a day. As you do it consistently over time, the loneliness you experience becomes the doorway to a rich connection with yourself. Taking the three precious pills will help you overcome feelings of loneliness and loss.

ཕ་འི་ག་དུ་ལ་ཁ་དཀར་དཀ་ཁ། །

ཡུག་ཁ་ནི་ཁྲི་ཁ་འདི་ཁ་དག །

 རེ་ག་ཁ་ནི་རྐྱ་ཁི་ཆེ་ད་ཁ་འཛེ་ག །

རྒྱ་འུ་མ་རྐྱ་ཁ་ཆེ་ག་ཁ་ད།།

Deluded ignorance naturally clears

Like the sun shining in a dark place.

The king of innate awareness
arrives at his own place

Like a prince taking his throne.

—from *The Twenty-One Nails,*
a Bön dzogchen text

CHAPTER 6

Nourishing Your Inner Being

I spend a lot of time throughout the year traveling to teach. Early one morning a few months ago I found myself once again standing on a shuttle bus between airport terminals. I could easily have spent that time feeling impatient to get to my destination. Instead, I closed my eyes and went into the familiar place of stillness, where I was no longer draining myself. The more deeply I rested in stillness, the more I could feel my internal battery recharging. The more warmth I felt, the more joy stirred within me. I began to smile.

When I opened my eyes, I noticed that a woman across from me was watching me. I sensed that she recognized I was doing some form of meditation. She closed her eyes, and by the time we arrived at the gate, she, too, was smiling.

Whenever and wherever you feel you are losing your vitality, life force, and soul, you can take a moment to sense which elemental quality you need most. You can go first into stillness, silence, and spaciousness in order to interrupt the negative pattern that is depleting you. Once you feel that the pattern has been interrupted, you have begun to protect yourself. You can go even deeper and rest in the warmth you discover there. You retrieve the quality you need simply by recognizing its presence in open awareness.

It is my advice to nourish your inner being in this way, several times a day. Whenever possible, do this in a natural setting. Connect to the earth and feel its stability. Sit by a lake, connecting with the sense of ease and comfort of water. Bask in the warmth of the sun, feeling its rays awakening your internal joy.

Retrieving the elements does not necessarily mean traveling far or doing elaborate meditation practices. No matter where you are, you can simply tune in to unbounded space, discover the quality that is already there, and feel nourished by it. Close your eyes, look within, and connect with stillness, silence, and spaciousness. You will discover that you *are* that infinite space. By bringing your attention to that space, you can receive from it all the nourishment you need.

Charging Your Battery

In a way, keeping your soul well nourished is like keeping the battery of a smart phone charged. There are certain steps you can take to avoid draining a phone's battery too quickly. For example, when an iPhone has many applications running in the background, the battery runs down faster, so it's best to turn off those apps when not using them. In similar fashion, you have a lot of unnecessary applications running in the background in your life. These are all the negative thoughts and emotions that are draining your energy even when you are not consciously engaging with them. As soon as you connect with stillness, silence, and spaciousness, you are effectively turning off these applications and no longer draining your internal battery.

You also need to plug in and charge your smart phone regularly. If you don't, the battery will be depleted and you will no longer be able to rely on the phone when you most need it. In the same way, you need to plug in regularly to the warmth of your inner source in order to keep your internal battery charged. By resting in the inner refuge, not only are you not draining your battery, you are charging it. When your battery stays charged, all the elemental qualities are available to you when you need them. What is magical is that you can be charging your battery even as you are drawing from it. Anytime you face challenges, you can go to the inner refuge where you are charging your battery and feel supported.

Use challenging moments as a reminder to plug in. For example, imagine that your car breaks down on the highway in the middle of the night. It's cold, it's raining, and you're alone in a remote spot where you can't call for help. Let the raindrops remind you of water's healing qualities. The motionlessness of your car, the silence of your surroundings, and the expanse of empty road can remind you to connect to stillness, silence, and spaciousness. If you can connect in that way, you will find peace amid challenges, and at the same time, find solutions to your problems.

At those times in your life when you feel no joy, if you connect with the inner refuge, joy is available to you. Joy does not distinguish between places or situations. It's only your ego that labels circumstances as undesirable or unfair: *Why me? This isn't supposed to happen to me.* As soon as you think that way, joy is eclipsed.

Having Trust

Security and connectedness are present even in the rockiest moments. Ease and comfort are available to you in the most uncomfortable circumstances. Bliss, freedom, flexibility, and openness—the elemental qualities are always available to you.

The question is, can you trust that they are available and that you can access them? When you are feeling a lot of pain, can you trust that you can close your eyes, connect with the space within, and feel a glimmer of comfort or joy? Once you find that comfort, can you be with it? Can you breathe into that feeling and stay with it longer? It's human nature to dwell on our problems. But if you can become a little more familiar with positive qualities, the next time you face a similar challenge, you will have a different response. You will know where to turn, and you will trust the support within you.

A Change of Habit

Changing our familiar habitual responses can seem difficult at first. One common excuse is *I don't have the time.* I am constantly hearing this mantra from Westerners. They think a lack of time is a reasonable excuse, but it really makes no sense, especially when it comes to nourishing one's inner being. We all seem to have the time to worry and dwell on negative thoughts, and yet we don't find the time to charge our batteries. Consider using the time you would normally devote to being worried and stressed to nourishing your inner being instead.

How do we normally fill our time? Imagine it is Monday morning and your full-blown pain body is activated.

You commute to work, enter the workplace, assume your professional identity, and confront the frenetic energy of a full schedule and all the co-workers or customers around you. You haven't taken any specific action to feel dragged down physically, emotionally, and mentally: your alarm clock, the commute, and the workplace have done this for you. But they only drain you because you allow them to, and because you think it's normal to experience Monday morning in this way. For some people, Monday morning extends into Tuesday, Wednesday, and Thursday. Even Sunday can feel like Monday morning if you spend all day worrying about the week ahead.

Another habitual response involves our often-unacknowledged expectations of friends, co-workers, and family members. We think, *I can't believe they did that!* Whenever you pursue a thought like that, you allow pain to interfere with your life. You are spending personal time activating emotions that drain your energy and block access to your elemental essences. By feeding your negativity, you sever your connection with the deep, beautiful silence that is always present within you. You lose the support of the positive elemental qualities.

Sometimes pain speech becomes a mantra. We become fixated on thoughts like *This is terrible. What am I going to do?* When pain talks with pain, however, nothing gets resolved. So stop the dialogue and give your full attention to connecting to stillness, silence, and spaciousness. Go into nature, if possible. Give your mind a break. Sit in the inner refuge for 15 minutes. You are likely to feel much better. One of my students described how well giving herself a break like this had worked for her:

> I spent the last 48 hours at the airport. In that
> situation I could easily have been consumed with

emotions that are destructive. Instead, I did informal practice. All the delays, canceled flights, and bad weather became manageable. They were just what they were. No anger, no worry, no big deal. I was calm around fellow passengers and flight attendants, who actually thanked me for my ability to handle the disruption. I arrived safely, happy to return to my husband, who was happy that I was not stressed from travel.

How often can you notice your negativity as it arises, and when it does, commit to taking the three precious pills? How often will you take a few minutes to enter into stillness, silence, and spaciousness? Meditation practice is about becoming familiar with the inner refuge, not just on the meditation cushion but in your day-to-day life as well.

Spontaneous Warmth

The qualities of the five elements feed your inner being and your soul. Allow time to be nourished by them. If you sit for half an hour with the experience of being complete just as you are in this moment, and you practice that every day for a week or more, you may soon find yourself happy for no reason. To your surprise and delight, joy or another elemental quality may spontaneously arise. One of my students described how a normally unpleasant situation had, through practice, transformed into something enjoyable:

In my informal practice I have had moments when a situation that would normally trigger fear and constriction in me instead triggers openness and bliss. Now I look forward to seeing the things that I feared. I feel much more aware with people in general, and I can feel warmth radiating from my heart outward into the space around me when I am in meetings and at lunch or dinner. In the past I often found I was too empathetic, and lost my sense of space and merged with another person's world. It was probably my ego trying too hard to belong. Now I feel more centered, yet still very open and connected to others. Better still, I feel the outflow of warm, loving energy.

Another student wrote of his surprise at his sudden positive response during an argument with his partner:

My anger was rising very strongly. Feeling this solid fighting energy, I turned my back to her. Suddenly I saw my anger, as if watching it from a balcony. Without even realizing it, the teachings spontaneously popped up in my mind—no words, just a feeling. In an instant I felt extremely peaceful and humorous. I smiled at my partner in a loving way, and the argument immediately dissolved. Probably a small step for humanity but a big step for me! Another time while practicing, a spontaneous rush of love rose up and filled the room, with absolutely no effort on my part.

Familiarity with the practice transforms your normal daily experiences. When the sky is clear of clouds, the sun shines and you feel its warmth. When you rest deeply in stillness, silence, and spaciousness, warmth spontaneously arises. Take every opportunity to feel that warmth, rest in it, and become more familiar with it. Take every moment to nourish and heal your inner being. Simply by being aware of the essential quality of an element, your battery is charged. Later, in times of need, you will be delighted to discover that healing qualities will surface without any effort.

In the end, you will have a deeper sense of who you are—a sense of feeling complete, alert, joyful, playful, creative. All these qualities must be awakened in you if you are to be the best of who you are. When the elemental qualities awaken in you, you recognize the fullness and completeness of your healthy, balanced soul.

Self-Guided Meditations: Nourishing Your Inner Being

The formal and informal practices that follow assume some familiarity with and connection to the inner refuge. If you are unable to access the inner refuge, the subtle warmth that arises from your connection with the three precious pills can also serve as the source of healing elemental qualities. Doing these practices daily will support you in feeling vital and fully restored. The fruits of these practices ripen naturally and spontaneously. They come from awareness of being and not from doing and striving. Trust and allow the practices to unfold naturally.

Formal Practice

Sit comfortably with legs crossed, spine straight, and chest open. If your physical condition does not permit such a posture, choose any upright sitting position that is comfortable, open, and uplifting.

Inhale deeply through both nostrils, hold your breath for a moment, and then exhale slowly and fully.

Repeat three times. As you exhale, release any tension and settle.

Draw your attention to your body from the crown of your head to the soles of your feet. Become aware of the stillness of your body. Your body is already still, but are you fully aware of that stillness? Rest in awareness of stillness. As the experience deepens, become aware of simply being. The nature of being is unbounded, indestructible, filled with potential, beyond death, beyond birth, beyond aging, beyond all changes. Just rest there.

Listen to the silence. You are silent in this moment, but are you aware of the silence? Rest in clear awareness of silence. It is beautiful, nourishing, peaceful.

Draw your attention to your heart. The nature of your heart and mind is always clear and open, but are you aware of that openness? Abide now in this vast spaciousness.

As you rest deeply in stillness, silence, and spaciousness, you are no longer depleting yourself.

As you continue to rest in the space of being, another, deeper space reveals itself: the space of inner refuge, where your pain begins to dissolve and you start to feel a sense of well-being. Feel the unbounded sacred space, infinite awareness, and genuine warmth.

Resting in the inner refuge, bring to mind a pain-related obstacle that is causing you to lose your soul, energy, and vitality. Allow the experience without judging, criticizing, or getting caught up in stories about it. As you host the experience with warmth, it begins to dissipate. Be aware of the dissolution. Simply allow it.

In the space where the obstacle has dissolved, you can discover the elemental quality you most need, whether related to earth, water, fire, air, or space. The moment you feel a connection to this quality, you are nourishing your soul with it.

If you are nourishing your soul with earth: There is warmth in the recognition of the earth element, in its qualities of strength, groundedness, solidity, and security. Feel the warmth of connection. This will occur naturally as you rest in the space of inner refuge and allow the quality to emerge. As the quality of earth arises, allow its warmth to permeate your body, nourishing your skin, bones, blood, muscles, and organs. Every cell of your body resonates with the warmth of connectedness. In this moment, your inner being is nurtured by earth.

If you are nourishing your soul with water: Within the infinite space of inner refuge, can you notice a sense of comfort, fluidity, and ease of being? Be aware of these qualities, and let a deep sense of comfort pervade your body. As you rest deeply, any blockages will naturally release. Allow the essence of the water element to saturate your mind, your field of energy, your body, and any places in your life where you have felt its absence. As you rest in connection with the water element, let its fluidity and comfort nurture your inner being, heal your pain, and nourish your soul.

If you are nourishing your soul with fire: When the qualities of inner fire—warmth, joy, enthusiasm, energy—arise in your experience, allow yourself to be fed by this sense of vitality. There is no need to produce these qualities. Just remain open and let them arise. As you feel these healing qualities, be aware of them. Experience the blissful warmth of the fire element as it radiates throughout your body. Being aware of and connected to this warmth, you are nourished by it.

If you are nourishing your soul with air: When the freely moving air element arises within the inner refuge, recognize that it is lifting and dispersing your negativity and bringing you to a place of playfulness and flexibility. Enjoy this uplifting, essential energy with every breath. Feel a deep sense of freedom nourishing all the cells of your body. Allow this sense of freedom to expand into your environment, pervading the natural world and all beings. Rest in this uplifted quality.

If you are nourishing your soul with space: The space element is accommodating and open. It cannot be destroyed or changed by any force. The essence of your mind, too, is open, accommodating, changeless, and indestructible. Are you aware of the vast openness that is your true nature? This awareness is not experienced as thought. It is a light that illuminates the truth of your being. Have confidence in it. At the moment when awareness dawns and illuminates the space of being, you are nourishing your soul.

Spend at least 10 to 15 minutes feeling deeply connected with the elemental quality you are retrieving. The longer you can maintain awareness of it, the more your practice will mature. If you lose awareness of the element you are working with, reconnect by bringing your attention back to stillness, silence, and spaciousness.

Dedicate the merit of your practice by bringing to mind this intention: *In liberating my own being, may I benefit others.*

Informal Practice

Each day, extend the nourishing experience of your formal meditation practice by engaging in the informal practice that follows. If you do this five times a day for at least two minutes at a time, the challenges in your life will more readily become opportunities to replenish your soul.

Many times when we are engaged in activity, we either disconnect from ourselves or resort to unnecessary effort to accomplish our task. Instead, you can practice not draining yourself. When you become aware of trying too hard, shift your attention and connect with the stillness of your body. When you get caught up in negative internal dialogue, shift your attention to your inner silence. When you notice that your mind is agitated, connect with the spaciousness of your mind.

Remembering to connect with the inner refuge in any circumstance is meditation in action. Take every opportunity to notice and connect with the elemental essences. For example, if you are feeling shaky, let that feeling remind you to connect with stillness, silence, and spaciousness, and discover stability and be nourished by it.

Any moment can serve as a reminder to engage in informal practice. We can find opportunities while standing in line at the bank or post office, riding public transportation, driving in rush-hour traffic, or even sitting in a dentist's chair. The most difficult places you encounter are often the best places to practice, because those are the places where you drain yourself the most.

For additional support in your practice, I have recorded a guided meditation focused on the practice of Retrieving by Taking Inner Refuge. To access this recording, visit www. hayhouse.com/download and enter the Product ID 2190 and download code ebook. If you have any trouble accessing the meditation audio, please contact Hay House Customer Care by phone—US (800) 654-5126 or INTL CC+(760) 431-7695—or visit www.hayhouse.com/contact.

ཁ་ཡ་ད་ཡ་ས་ཤ་ཚིག་ཡ་བཞེག །

རེ་ག་ཡེ་རྒྱ་ཡ་ཨོ་རྒྱབ་ས་ཤ་ཚིག །

Like a lotus emerging from the mud,

The king of innate awareness emerges
from the inner chamber.

—from *The Twenty-One Nails*,
a Bön dzogchen text

CHAPTER 7

Nourishing Your Physical Body

I believe that in the future, it will be routine to connect with our inner resources to promote physical healing. Awareness practices will be recognized for their efficacy in addressing health issues and will be prescribed. Countless practitioners over the centuries have depended on meditation to transform negative emotions and heal physical maladies. The openness, awareness, and warmth of a healthy soul are natural antidotes to physical illness and pain, and may even foster longevity.

In recent decades, Western science has demonstrated this powerful connection between mind and body. Research suggests that our mental and emotional states, along with social, spiritual, and behavioral factors, play a major role in physical illness. Poor emotional health is associated with a weakened immune system, making us more likely to succumb to colds and other infections. And disturbing emotions have been linked to a wide variety of physical problems, from headaches, insomnia, extreme fatigue, back pain, gastrointestinal disorders, and changes in weight or appetite to high blood pressure, heart palpitations, chest pain, and shortness of breath.[1] Anger is a known risk factor for cardiovascular disease and strokes.

Nearly all of us have experienced the powerful connection between mind and body, discovering firsthand what researchers have found: that mind-body therapies can help ease chronic pain and symptoms of disease, sharpen our psychological functioning, and improve our quality of life.[2] Just as you take prescription medicines to relieve particular symptoms, you can use the limitless capacity of mind and bring the five elemental healing qualities to areas of the body where those qualities are missing. In this way, soul retrieval can feed your life force and promote profound healing.

As you become more familiar with retrieving the elemental qualities you need from nature, the inner refuge, and your relationships, you will be able to use all the practices set out in this book for your own healing. Grounded in traditional Bön teachings, these practices bring nourishment to your body as well as healing to your soul.

One Medicine for All Ills

The inner refuge, with its qualities of spaciousness, luminosity, and warmth, is potent medicine. I have witnessed the physical benefits of the inner refuge repeatedly in myself as well as in my students. On a recent retreat, after I guided the healing practice described later in this chapter, many participants said their physical symptoms had eased. The variety of changes they reported was impressive: reduced lower back pain, improved eyesight, relief from chronic bronchitis. One student even found that sensation had returned to a scarred area where there had previously been no feeling at all. Several people said their chronic pain had disappeared altogether.

Ancient Buddhist scriptures describe primordial awareness as the medicine for treating and healing pain or disease. Most Western scholars have interpreted the words *pain* and *disease* in these texts as meaning psychological pain. But the texts are clearly referring to the healing of physical pain and disease as well as emotional suffering.

Conventional treatments often play an important—even life-saving—role in symptom relief and healing, but if you can harness the power of practices that connect with primordial awareness, you have the potential to go directly to the root of physical pain and illness. It is my belief that in many cases of spontaneous healing, inner awareness is a central factor. According to the ancient texts, the healing qualities of the five elements and the five wisdoms are naturally present in awareness.

The internal elements themselves are associated with various organs: the earth element is associated with the spleen, the water element with the kidneys, the fire element with the liver, the air element with the lungs, and the space element with the heart. As the elements come into balance within us, they sustain the healthy functioning of these essential organs.

Shifting Attention

As a teacher, I feel it is important to remind students that the primary goal of meditation practice is to reinforce our connection with the nature of mind. So when we practice with pain, disease, or anything else that interferes with our open awareness, we do so to become more familiar with the inner refuge and stabilize our experience of it, and through that familiarity to heal our soul. Physical healing, when it occurs, is a welcome byproduct. But even if our physical ailments cannot be completely cured, our relationship with pain and sickness can be healed. In this way, pain and sickness can be a support for our spiritual growth rather than a hindrance.

When pain is used as an opportunity to reinforce a connection with stillness, silence, and spaciousness, not only does the pain begin to lessen but it becomes the doorway to spiritual practice. The more we practice opening our attention and hosting the pain rather than contracting around it, the stronger this more expansive sense of self becomes.

The Producer of the Pain

I want to make a distinction between pain and the pain identity. If we do not clear the pain identity—remove the root cause of pain or sickness—our practice will be no more effective than taking aspirin every day for a tension headache. Without addressing the cause, the symptoms will just keep coming back.

When you suffer with pain, it is because there is an "I" experiencing that pain. In grasping our sense of self, we perpetuate our suffering. So with the first inner refuge, as we connect with unbounded sacred space in the presence of our pain, the "I"—the ego self that contracts around the pain—loosens its grip. Our identity as a sick person who is suffering becomes less solid. As we continue to rest in the space of being, the sense of "I" dissolves into space, and in that moment we recognize that we are not our pain; we are the open space of being itself. That is our true nature.

When I moved to the United States many years ago, I remember watching a television program that showed an image of our beautiful planet Earth, a photograph taken from outer space by the crew of Apollo 17. The world looked so small, Texas even smaller. My hometown of Houston was nonexistent. I had studied logic for years in the monastery to come to a direct understanding of the dissolution of self, and this one image brought me there effortlessly. If Houston doesn't exist, then I don't exist, and if I don't exist, then what is the problem?

Have you ever listened to someone complain about their difficulties and become impatient with them because it was clear to you that the person was the problem, not what they were complaining about? It is easier to see that the person is the problem when that person is someone other than you. As a teacher, I am often approached by students who want to talk about their difficulties. If I were to exclaim, "The truth is, I think *you* are the problem!" they would surely think I wasn't listening to them or didn't care about their very real life situation—a terrible teacher, right? So it is better for me to at least tell them, "Yes, that's interesting; it sounds like there is something to what you are saying." But here in our practice, we want to clear that "I," the creator of the problem. Doing so not only relieves our discomfort but also makes it less likely that the pain, blockage, or illness will return.

We also want to clear the "I" that is not so much complaining as continually trying to offer good ideas to fix the problem. This smart ego seems to be part of the solution but is actually part of the problem, a producer of pain. It doesn't question its existence, and smart or not, the ego is never satisfied. It never has a sense that everything is fine.

No matter what you do or what happens in life, your ego will find something that needs improvement.

I have a friend who always contradicts what I say. If I'm trying on a pair of glasses in the store and say, "These are quite good," he will respond, "Yes, but those other frames are better." I imagine that if I told him instead, "These glasses aren't as good as those other ones," he would respond, "No, the ones you have on are better." By contrast, my own teacher, Yongdzin Tenzin Namdak Rinpoche, will agree with 90 percent of whatever you say. "Nice glasses? Okay, yes, they are nice." "Terrible glasses? You are right." If he sees you are in need of life-changing guidance, he will be sure to offer it. But nearly everything else is fine with him. We could all benefit from this kind of egoless acceptance, particularly of our own pain.

As we connect with the first inner refuge, the "I" clears, and we begin to realize the truth of who we are. We already *are* the space and awareness, but that has been obscured. The moment we become more open, we are also more open to our pain. Since we are no longer defending our contracted identity, the suffering dissipates and we experience a sense of greater freedom.

The second inner refuge—the light of awareness—brings clarity and presence. Our pain no longer seems so solid, and our pain identity begins to loosen and dissolve as we rest in unbounded spaciousness. Awareness of the spaciousness within both the pain and the pain identity liberates the energy invested in the pain. Now the energy becomes available for healing, and even if the impulse to contract arises, we do not give in to it.

With the third inner refuge, the warmth is embodied and can now support positive physical change. One of my students wrote of her success in bringing warmth to both the long-standing pain in her spine and the pain identity, the producer of the pain:

> Usually, by this time I would be flat on my back for a week with ice bags and pain pills—and that's not happening. I find myself feeling warm compassion when the pain identity speaks, so I'm not blocking or ignoring or repressing the pain. I let it be as it is, hold it in warm attention, wrap it up in a warm blanket, and give it an energetic hot toddy. Pain doesn't seem so serious anymore.

Taking the three refuges in sequence, first we address the producer of the pain, then the energetic dimension of the pain, and then the pain itself. Instead of a pain body, or pain identity, there is the body of emptiness, or unbounded spaciousness: this is the first refuge. Instead of pain speech, there is the body of light, or infinite awareness—the second refuge. Instead of pain mind, there is the body of great bliss, or genuine warmth—the third refuge. In actuality, there is no sequence to the inner refuge; space always contains the qualities of light and warmth. But when your connection to the inner refuge is blocked and obscured, following a step-by-step progression of opening can be helpful in recognizing and overcoming your habitual patterns.

Pain as Appearance: Seeing with the Wisdom Eye

By now you are aware that spaciousness, light, and warmth are present in every moment. These three aspects of inner refuge are found in every sensory experience, in every thought that goes through your mind—and even in places you would never imagine finding these qualities, such as mental confusion, negative emotions, physical pain, and disease. When you open to unbounded sacred space, you can discover light within darkness, solutions within conflict. But to see in this way, you need the wisdom eye, the healing eye—not the eye of the one who is producing the pain.

Having the correct eye requires a shift in perspective. Of course, it is easy to experience spaciousness, light, and warmth in a beautiful flower or a majestic sunrise. But can you experience these qualities within fear? Even within the feeling of fear, there is space. When fear arises, rather than leading you away from yourself into reactivity and negative thoughts, it can become a doorway to your essential self. Fear and beauty both arise from the same mother space, the source of everything. The five elemental qualities, the five pure lights, and the five wisdoms of the enlightened state (see Table 3, page 127) are present even in fear.

The ever-present, unbounded sacred space of your nature is beyond distinctions of beauty or ugliness, pain or pleasure. Just as fear can drive you away from connection with your essential nature, beauty, too, can pull you away from it. And just as fear can lead you back to your essential nature, so can beauty. When you see a beautiful flower, you may believe that the beauty lies in the flower and not in you. Regarding the flower as the source of that beauty reinforces your sense of yourself as one who is lacking—in this instance, lacking beauty. But the wisdom eye recognizes that the beauty of the flower is also the beauty of who you are: both arise from the same source, the inner refuge. Everything is of the same nature.

So what happens when we perceive pain with the wisdom eye? Normally when we have pain, we experience that we *are* the pain: *I am hurting.* But when you identify with the space, light, and warmth of the inner refuge, then even when blockages and pain are present, you recognize that you are fundamentally pure. In the dzogchen teachings the lotus is used to illustrate our fundamentally pure nature. The lotus grows in water, and although the roots lie in the mud at the bottom of a murky pond, the blossom rests on the water's surface, its petals unblemished and pure. When you are fully present in pain, can you feel your lotus nature?

Pain is appearance. Blockages, numbness, and discomfort are appearances. The thoughts and stressful speech you have about your pain are appearances. All the challenging situations you experience are also appearances. No matter what appears in it, unbounded sacred space is unchanging. Can you recognize your unbounded nature? As we've been practicing, stillness of the body, silence of speech, and spaciousness of mind are the three doors that lead to the recognition of our unbounded nature. This recognition cuts the root of suffering. When the root is cut, no appearance can delude or disturb you. By going for inner refuge and becoming familiar with the truth of your unbounded nature, you come to feel strong enough and brave enough to journey to the very heart of appearances, rather than continually running away from them. Discovering the space, light, and warmth in the presence of appearance is healing.

When pain is your challenge, if you can access the inner refuge and rest there, you will gain confidence that you are not your pain. Furthermore, your suffering will transform. Pain will no longer define your whole existence, and positive qualities like love, humor, and joy will become available to you.

In the midst of pain, remember that you always have the choice to connect to stillness, silence, and spaciousness, and rest in the inner refuge. As you rest there, open awareness can clear disturbing thoughts and emotions as well as soothe physical pain. How much is your life guided by light and awareness, and how much is it driven by reactivity and denial? The inner refuge is your unfailing support in any moment. Let it be your best friend.

There are many practices, both ancient and modern, that promote healing, among them positive attention, visualization, and guided imagery. Most rely on mental activity as the method of healing. Loving-kindness meditation, for example, involves repeating intentions like *May all beings be happy* and *May all beings be healthy.* Such practices can be particularly beneficial when they support a connection with the space, awareness, and warmth of the inner refuge. But it's important to remember that conceptually based practices are only a tool. They point us to an experience, but they are not the experience itself. If you can connect directly with the inner refuge and its qualities of spaciousness, awareness, and warmth, mental activity is not necessary for healing.

The Power of Warmth

How you relate to your physical discomfort determines how it affects you. Do you see pain as an enemy, or do you relate to your discomfort with warmth and kindness? Unfortunately, most of us see pain as an enemy. Without the light and warmth of the sun, trees and flowering plants will fail to flourish. Without awareness and warmth toward your body, you, too, will fail to flourish.

There is a saying in Tibetan: We touch the area of the body that is in pain again and again. We habitually give not only too much attention to the places that hurt but also the wrong kind of attention. We can't stop talking and thinking about our pain—criticizing, judging, and rejecting it, and suffering from it as a result. When you feel pain in your knee, you think, *I can't stand this pain!* Then you start to think, *I can't stand my knee!* If your thoughts persist in this direction, eventually you can't stand yourself or your life. In visiting and revisiting our physical pain, we add emotional pain to our discomfort. And yet, if we ignore our pain, it is likely to complain even louder for attention.

In our practice, instead of ignoring or denying pain, we open to it. Instead of trying to suppress pain, we become aware of it. Instead of disliking pain, we bring warmth to it.

Our physical pain benefits from our warmth and kindness. Kindness begins to undo our aversion or denial. Can you sit with your pain like a loving mother sitting with her ailing child? Nestled in his mother's familiar arms, the child receives protection, attention, and love. Neither the child nor the mother needs to do anything special. Resting in that connection, both are nourished.

The part of the body in pain immediately responds to the warmth of our attention. No longer the object of our aversion or fear, the pain receives the fullness of our presence. It is acknowledged, respected, and cared for. As the pain responds to this attention, the process of healing begins.

A Practice for Physical Healing

The meditation practice at the end of this chapter is for healing physical pain. We begin the practice by focusing on the three precious pills of stillness, silence, and spaciousness, to gather the wandering mind and connect with the inner refuge. As we settle into the practice, we rest in the qualities of the inner refuge: spaciousness, awareness, and warmth.

Then we draw the warmth of our attention to our physical pain or discomfort and host the pain like a loving mother comforting her child. This warmth, which naturally arises from a deep connection with the inner refuge, is essential for healing our relationship with pain—a relationship that, as we have discovered, is often constricted and conflicted. As we bring loving-kindness to the pain, the constriction begins to release.

We then shift our focus to the very heart of the pain itself. Here we connect deeply with stillness, silence, and spaciousness, and awaken the healing power of the inner refuge. The power of the unbounded spaciousness of the first refuge dissolves the pain identity. The power of the pure light of awareness of the second refuge frees and activates subtle healing energy. The five pure lights associated with the five elements and the five wisdom qualities (see Table 3 on the next page) become available to us. With the third refuge, the power of the genuine warmth arising from the union of openness and awareness transforms the expression of the pain. In some instances, the pain may even disappear altogether.

Table 3: The Five Pure Lights and Associated Elements and Wisdoms

Light	Element	Wisdom·
Yellow	Earth	Mirrorlike wisdom
Blue	Water	All-accomplishing wisdom
Red	Fire	Discriminating wisdom
Green	Air	Wisdom of equanimity
White	Space	Wisdom of emptiness

* Descriptions of the five wisdoms appear in Chapter 2 on page 51.

Whether the warmth you feel in your practice arises from a deep connection with the three precious pills or from the immense power of the inner refuge, you receive great benefit. The warmth arising naturally from your open attention gives a spacious, luminous hug to your pain, blockage, or illness.

As you practice, it is important that you not exert effort. In other words, do not try to create a state of mind or make something happen. Instead, simply be aware of your authentic presence. Your presence is not something you create; it emerges naturally when you are open, aware, and warm. Trying to be something other than what you are is an obscuration. Trying reinforces the pain identity, whereas openness releases it. If you are not open, and you try to generate a feeling of loving-kindness, your kindness may not have much impact. You will be imposing an idea of kindness on yourself or others, rather than expressing genuine open-heartedness.

It is one thing to say, "Practice without effort," but can you do it? Begin by connecting as deeply as possible with stillness, silence, and spaciousness, and resting there. Allow any experiences that arise, hosting them without changing anything, and as they release, remain present. Feel the warmth of connection, comfort, peacefulness, or joy—whatever arises for you. As you give space, awareness, and warmth to the pain, blockage, or sickness, it will release. As it releases, the liveliness and warmth of loving-kindness emerge, just as a baby smiles when its mother reappears after a separation.

It's amazing how quickly change can happen when you fully allow it. A few years ago I founded The 3 Doors, a program of life-transforming practices based on the teachings of inner refuge. Over and over, students undergoing this training have told me that while previously they would use effort to try to make beneficial changes in their lives, once they discovered the power of openness and awareness, many changes happened spontaneously.

One sign that your practice is too effortful is that instead of getting better, your pain gets worse. That means pain is focusing on pain. A good sign that you are practicing with open awareness is that your pain lessens and you feel increased comfort or joy. The inner-refuge practice is about abiding in space, light, and warmth, and trusting in the power of that to bring about positive transformation.

The inner refuge is vaster than any pain that might occupy it. Knowing this, we are encouraged to host any experience within that space. A couple of years ago I fell while riding my bicycle and dislocated my shoulder. At the emergency room they told me that I could wait an hour for the anesthesiologist to arrive, or they could push my arm back in place immediately without anesthesia. I thought, *Wow, this is a great opportunity to host my pain in the space of inner refuge!* So I told them, "Okay, do it right now." I can't say I felt no pain at all, but by hosting and allowing the pain in spaciousness, awareness, and warmth, I suffered far less than I would have guessed. The pain was manageable, and the whole experience was enlivening.

Self-Guided Meditations: Nourishing Your Physical Body

Formal Practice

For best results in healing physical pain, physical blocks, or disease, devote at least 30 minutes a day to the practice of giving a spacious, luminous, warm hug to your pain. In this practice, you will be focusing on the specific area of your body that is affected. If your discomfort is not confined to a specific location, focus more globally on the body system or disorder affecting you. Continue to practice with this focus until your experience of pain has eased or you feel that your relationship to the pain has been transformed in a beneficial way. Move on to another physical issue only after you have experienced lasting positive results with the first.

Sit comfortably with your legs crossed, spine straight, and chest open. If your physical condition does not permit such a posture, choose any upright position that is comfortable.

Allow your body to relax. Draw your attention inward.

Preparation

First refuge: Feel the stillness in your body. Connect with that stillness and rest in it. Gradually feel and be aware of inner stillness, the stillness of being. Through that inner stillness, be aware of unbounded sacred space, the first inner refuge. In Bön, this dimension of being is referred to as the *dharmakaya,* the body of emptiness.

Second refuge: Listen and hear the silence within. Feel and connect with the inner silence. Allow yourself to rest deeply in it. As you rest, connect with the presence of awareness—the second inner refuge. In Bön, this dimension of infinite awareness is the *sambhogakaya,* the body of light.

Third refuge: Bring your attention to the space within and around your heart. Connect with the spaciousness and become like the open sky. Be aware of the warmth that is naturally present. Allow this warmth to emerge fully. This is the warmth of the union of openness and awareness—the third inner refuge. In Bön, this dynamic energy is the *nirmanakaya,* the body of great manifestation.

Healing the Physical Body

Now gradually draw your attention to the specific area of your body where you experience any blockage, discomfort, pain, or sickness. Bring your attention to that location with loving-kindness and care, as a healer would attend to a patient, or a loving mother would comfort her child.

Your physical pain or illness needs the warmth of loving-kindness and care. Through your attention, you bring the healing power of openness, connectedness, and warmth to your body where it is needed. Allow time to feel this.

Now shift your focus to the center of your affliction.

First refuge: As you rest in stillness, be aware of the unbounded sacred space that begins to come alive in the physical location of your affliction. This sense of opening can not only unblock and clear the pain but also dissolve the producer of the pain, the pain identity that has been avoiding, clinging to, or disconnecting

130

from the pain on a very subtle level. Allow this power-ful opening.

Second refuge: Now, within the deep silence the light of awareness arises. Your pain, blockage, or sick-ness is alive with awareness. Experience the pure light of awareness radiating throughout this space. The light contains five colors—yellow, blue, red, green, and white—representing the pure energies of the five wis-doms and the five elemental essences. Feel the healing energies of the inner lights. Feel your darkness, pain, and sickness clearing.

Third refuge: As you connect deeply with the warmth of the union of openness and awareness, bring this warmth to the space within and around your pain, discomfort, or blockage. Just as when the sun shines, and its warmth begins to melt the frost on a window, when you rest in open awareness the genuine warmth of connection begins to restructure pain and sickness. Your awareness of the warmth activates the process of physical healing.

Allow this energetic healing response. Rest in the healing warmth for as long as it remains.

Dedicate your practice to the welfare of others, particularly those who are experiencing pain, with the thought: *In liberating my own being, may I benefit others.*

Informal Practice

Throughout your day, as soon as you become aware that your pain mind is drawing negative atten-tion to your physical pain, blockage, or sickness, take the three precious pills. Connect with stillness, silence, and spaciousness. Instead of pushing away your pain, be open to it and host it in the spaciousness that be-comes available as you connect with stillness. Instead of complaining about the pain, be aware of it and host it in the light of awareness that becomes available as you connect with inner silence. Instead of spinning a story about your pain, accept the pain and host it in the inner warmth that becomes available as you connect with the spaciousness of mind.

Gradually allow both your pain identity and your physical pain to dissolve in the spaciousness, light, and warmth of the inner refuge.

You can do this informal practice at any time. You could devote 30 seconds or more to the practice during a short break between activities at work or at home. If you have a little more time—while sitting in the park or in a doctor's office, for example—spend a few minutes on the practice.

Unconsciously, you might be drawing negative attention to your pain hundreds of times a day. Therefore, commit to doing this informal exercise at least five times over the course of the day. As you become more familiar with the practice and feel its benefits, you will be inspired to increase the number of times per day that you do it.

Afterword

It is my hope that this book has brought you closer to meeting the resources you already have within you to retrieve your soul and lead a balanced and fulfilled life. We first considered how you lose your soul—lose the vital connection to the source within you. And then we explored ways to retrieve your soul—from nature, from relationships, and with the three precious pills of stillness, silence, and spaciousness. These are all ways of reconnecting to the inner refuge and retrieving the essential qualities you need. In embodying those qualities, you heal your soul.

Ultimately, there is only one cause of soul loss. The cause is ignorance—a fundamental misunderstanding of the truth of who you are. You are not alone in experiencing this: ignorance of our true nature is the root of all human suffering. Misunderstanding our true nature underlies every conflict that arises between individuals and between nations, and pervades every form of suffering we experience personally or collectively. Losing your connection to the source within means losing your connection not only to your own body and soul but also to the people you care about and to the natural world.

Just as there is only one cause of soul loss, there is only one cure: awareness. When you fully realize the truth of your nature—that you *are* the unbounded sacred space, infinite awareness, and genuine warmth within you—you achieve final liberation from suffering. Not only do you become the inner refuge but you also become a source of benefit to others. The power of awareness is such that every experience, even a negative one, is a doorway to awakening.

As you have seen throughout these pages, when you uncover the manifestations of your pain identity and your delusions—all that you *are not*—and you host them with kindness in the inner refuge, they dissolve. When who you are not releases, you experience a new sense of openness that may at first seem empty and unfamiliar. But when the light of awareness touches the sky of your being, you discover the treasure within. All the elemental essences are alive within you. As you embody these essential qualities, you are complete. You heal your soul.

The elemental qualities are always present, always available. As they arise in you, welcome them. Value them. Allow them to nourish you. Then extend to others the healing warmth you have received.

Soul retrieval is not a passive process. You will not retrieve your soul by sitting back and merely observing the flow of experience. At the same time, you cannot retrieve your soul by exerting effort. Basic to all the practices set out in this book is the notion of *allowing.* As you connect with inner stillness, silence, and spaciousness, and rest in the inner refuge, you simply *allow* the healing warmth that is always there to arise naturally. As this warmth arises, it energizes you, just as the heat of a stove causes the molecules of water in a teakettle to dance. The warmth of the inner refuge moves you to act for your own benefit and for the well-being of the world. As you trust in your connection to the inner refuge—to your genuine self—you are inspired to express love, compassion, joy, and equanimity to those around you.

Every formal meditation in the book ends with a dedication. It is a Bön tradition to offer the merit—the benefit—of our practice to all beings, especially to those who are suffering, so that they, too, may heal. Trust in your power to transform yourself and your life, and then at every opportunity, exercise this power on behalf of others.

It is my deepest wish that your life be perfectly fulfilled. You have my blessings and my prayers.

Tenzin Wangyal
Berkeley, California
December 2014

Endnotes

Preface

1. More information about the traditional practices and rituals of soul retrieval appears in the introduction to Tenzin Wangyal Rinpoche's book *Healing with Form, Energy, and Light: The Five Elements in Tibetan Shamanism, Tantra, and Dzogchen* (Ithaca, NY: Snow Lion Publications, 2002).

Introduction

1. *The Seven Mirrors of Dzogchen* (*rdzogs chen me long bdun pa*) in the Bön Kanjur (theg chen g.yung drung bon gyi bka' 'gyur), vol. 177, ed. Mongyal Lhasey Rinpoche (smon rgyal lha sras) (Chengdu: si khron zhing chen par khrun lte gnas par 'debs khang, 1999), 295–323.

2. "Posttraumatic Stress Disorder (PTSD)," MedicineNet.com, accessed July 31, 2014.

    See also Donald Edmondson et al., "Posttraumatic Stress Disorder Prevalence and Risk of Recurrence in Acute Coronary Syndrome Patients: A Meta-analytic Review," *PLoS ONE* 7, no. 6 (June 2012): e38915, doi:10.1371/journal.pone.0038915.

Chapter 1: Looking Closely at Your Life

1. In all cases where *The Twenty-One Nails* is listed as the source of a quotation, information is drawn from *The Twenty-One Nails: A Dzogchen Text from the Oral Transmission of Zhang Zhung*, trans. by Kurt Keutzer and Geshe Tenzin Wangyal (Shipman, VA: Ligmincha Institute, 2014).

2. "State of the American Workplace: Employee Engagement Insights for U.S. Business Leaders," 12–13, accessed April 30, 2014, http://www.gallup.com/services/178514/state-american-workplace.aspx.

Chapter 2: Retrieving from Nature

1. The nature spirits described in the Tibetan traditions include the *klu*, subterranean spirits associated with the water element; the *tsen*, associated with rocks; the *mela*, or fire spirits; the *nagas*, or water spirits; the *sadak*, or earth lords; and the *nyen*, or tree spirits. There are also said to be spirits in fields, spirits at the junctions of roads, and spirits of space.

Chapter 5: Overcoming Loneliness

1. John T. Cacioppo et al., "Loneliness as a Specific Risk Factor for Depressive Symptoms: Cross-Sectional and Longitudinal Analyses," *Psychology and Aging* 21, no. 1 (March 2006): 140–51, http://dx.doi.org/10.1037/0882-7974.21.1.140; John T. Cacioppo, Louise C. Hawkley, and Gary G. Berntson, "The Anatomy of Loneliness," *Current Directions in Psychological Science* 12, no. 3 (June 2003): 71–74, http://psychology.uchicago.edu/people/faculty/cacioppo/jtcreprints/chb03.pdf; Conor Ó Luanaigh and Brian A. Lawlor, "Loneliness and the Health of Older People," *International Journal of Geriatric Psychiatry* 23, no. 12 (June 2008): 1213–21, http://onlinelibrary.wiley.com/doi/10.1002/gps.2054/abstract.

Chapter 7: Nourishing Your Physical Body

1. "Mind/Body Connection: How Your Emotions Affect Your Health," FamilyDoctor.org, American Academy of Family Physicians, accessed April 30, 2014, http://familydoctor.org/familydoctor/en/prevention-wellness/emotional-wellbeing/mental-health/

mind-body-connection-how-your-emotions-affect-your-health
.printerview.html.

2. NIH Medline Plus, Winter 2008, 4, accessed April 30, 2014, http://
    www.nlm.nih.gov/medlineplus/magazine/issues/winter08/articles/
    winter08pg4.html.

Acknowledgments

I wish to express my deep, heartfelt devotion and gratitude to my teacher, Yongdzin Tenzin Namdak Rinpoche. Through his immeasurable generosity, kindness, and support, Yongdzin Rinpoche has been nourishing my soul for more than 40 years. It is from this connection that I am able to inspire and serve others through the writing of this book and in all of my other, ongoing efforts to preserve the Tibetan Bön teachings and traditions.

I am also very grateful to H. E. Menri Lopon Trinley Nyima Rinpoche, head instructor of Menri Monastery in Dolanji, India, for being open and available to answer my questions as they have arisen during the writing process.

I give special thanks to my wife, Khandro Tsering Wangmo, who with genuine openness and warmth has given me the space needed to freely dedicate my time to this work.

I thank Patty Gift of Hay House for her care and expertise in overseeing this book's completion. Through her great knowledge and years of experience in editing and publishing, Patty has enriched this book and increased its accessibility to Western readers. I am also grateful to Marcy Vaughn, who, by assisting in the editing process, lent her clear, warm voice to the publication. As the director of study and practice for Ligmincha International and the editor of three of my other books, she has a close knowledge of my teachings and the ability to loosen my writings from their habitual patterns.

I wish to thank Mark Dahlby and Andrew Lukianowicz, editors of my earlier books, who in generosity of spirit took the time to review the book in its early stages and offer valuable suggestions for improvement. I also thank Kurt Keutzer for his ready assistance with translations and bibliographic references.

The main person who deserves my deep acknowledgment is Polly Turner, who has put countless hours of work into editing this book with patience, kindness, and dedication. Through her very intuitive understanding of my core message, Polly has helped me to craft these words in the most direct, simple, and accessible way. Without her the book would not have been possible.

I also appreciate Sue Davis-Dill, executive director of Ligmincha Institute at Serenity Ridge, for her joyful support over the years in overseeing administrative matters related to all my publications, including the many foreign-language versions.

Finally, I wish to thank all the members of Ligmincha International who, through their enormous dedication to my work, help me to help others.

About the Author

Tenzin Wangyal Rinpoche is a recognized master of the Tibetan Bön Buddhist tradition. A respected teacher to students around the world, he is the founder of Ligmincha International, a worldwide organization dedicated to preserving the ancient Yungdrung Bön teachings of the Buddha Tonpa Shenrap, as well as the arts, sciences, language, and literature of Tibet and the ancient kingdom of Zhang Zhung. His books in English are *Awakening the Luminous Mind; Awakening the Sacred Body; Tibetan Sound Healing; Tibetan Yogas of Body, Speech, and Mind; The Tibetan Yogas of Dream and Sleep; Healing with Form, Energy, and Light; Wonders of the Natural Mind;* and *Unbounded Wholeness* (with Anne Klein).

Tenzin Wangyal Rinpoche resides in California with his wife and son. For information about Tenzin Rinpoche's activities, please visit www.ligmincha.org.

Hay House Titles of Related Interest

YOU CAN HEAL YOUR LIFE, the movie,
starring Louise Hay & Friends
(available as an online streaming video)
www.hayhouse.com/louise-movie

THE SHIFT, the movie,
starring Dr. Wayne W. Dyer
(available as an online streaming video)
www.hayhouse.com/the-shift-movie

• • •

THE END OF SUFFERING AND THE DISCOVERY OF HAPPINESS:
The Path of Tibetan Buddhism, by His Holiness the Dalai Lama

FEARLESS IN TIBET: The Life of the Mystic Tertön Sogyal,
by Matteo Pistono

LOVE YOUR ENEMIES: How to Break the Anger Habit & Be a
Whole Lot Happier, by Sharon Salzberg and Robert Thurman

A MINDFUL NATION: How a Simple Practice Can Help Us Reduce
Stress, Improve Performance, and Recapture the American Spirit,
by Congressman Tim Ryan

WHY MEDITATE?: Working with Thoughts and Emotions,
by Matthieu Ricard

All of the above are available at your local bookstore,
or may be ordered by contacting Hay House (see next page).

• • •

We hope you enjoyed this Hay House book. If you'd like to receive our online catalog featuring additional information on Hay House books and products, or if you'd like to find out more about the Hay Foundation, please contact:

Hay House, Inc., P.O. Box 5100, Carlsbad, CA 92018-5100
(760) 431-7695 or (800) 654-5126
(760) 431-6948 (fax) or (800) 650-5115 (fax)
www.hayhouse.com® • www.hayfoundation.org

———

Published in Australia by: Hay House Australia Pty. Ltd.,
18/36 Ralph St., Alexandria NSW 2015
Phone: 612-9669-4299 • *Fax:* 612-9669-4144
www.hayhouse.com.au

Published in the United Kingdom by: Hay House UK, Ltd.,
The Sixth Floor, Watson House, 54 Baker Street, London W1U 7BU
Phone: +44 (0)20 3927 7290 • *Fax:* +44 (0)20 3927 7291
www.hayhouse.co.uk

Published in India by: Hay House Publishers India,
Muskaan Complex, Plot No. 3, B-2, Vasant Kunj, New Delhi 110 070
Phone: 91-11-4176-1620 • *Fax:* 91-11-4176-1630
www.hayhouse.co.in

———

Access New Knowledge.
Anytime. Anywhere.

Learn and evolve at your own pace
with the world's leading experts.

www.hayhouseU.com

Listen. Learn. Transform.

Listen to the audio version of this book for FREE!

Live more consciously, strengthen your relationship with the Divine, and cultivate inner peace with world-renowned authors and teachers—all in the palm of your hand. With the *Hay House Unlimited* Audio app, you can learn and grow in a way that fits your lifestyle . . . and your daily schedule.

With your membership, you can:

- Embrace the power of your mind and heart, dive deep into your soul, rise above fear, and draw closer to Spirit.

- Explore thousands of audiobooks, meditations, immersive learning programs, podcasts, and more.

- Access exclusive audios you won't find anywhere else.

- Experience completely unlimited listening. No credits. No limits. No kidding.

Try for FREE!

Free e-newsletters from Hay House, the Ultimate Resource for Inspiration

Be the first to know about Hay House's free downloads, special offers, giveaways, contests, and more!

 Get exclusive excerpts from our latest releases and videos from *Hay House Present Moments.*

 Our *Digital Products Newsletter* is the perfect way to stay up-to-date on our latest discounted eBooks, featured mobile apps, and Live Online and On Demand events.

 Learn with real benefits! *HayHouseU.com* is your source for the most innovative online courses from the world's leading personal growth experts. Be the first to know about new online courses and to receive exclusive discounts.

 Enjoy uplifting personal stories, how-to articles, and healing advice, along with videos and empowering quotes, within *Heal Your Life.*

Sign Up Now!

Get inspired, educate yourself, get a complimentary gift, and share the wisdom!

Visit www.hayhouse.com/newsletters to sign up today!